Martha Merrill
Editor

Reference Services and Media

Reference Services and Media has been co-published simultaneously as *The Reference Librarian,* Number 65 1999.

Pre-publication
REVIEWS,
COMMENTARIES,
EVALUATIONS . . .

"**L**ibrarians looking for a contextual basis, background information and analysis of trends in electronic based reference services will find this publication very useful. In a series of contributed chapters edited by Martha Merrill, practitioners in the field share their knowledge and experiences in using media and computer based resources to provide reference services. While primarily directed at academic libraries, there is ample information that will also make this a useful resource for public libraries."

Tom Budlong, BA, MLn
Buckhead Branch Manager
Atlanta-Fulton Public Library

More pre-publication
REVIEWS, COMMENTARIES, EVALUATIONS . . .

"**I**n an age of very rapid development of electronic media, it can be easy to ignore or overlook the place of the human interface in the reference encounter. While each of these papers has approached the subject of media and reference in a unique way, the salient characteristic of this collection of papers is in their acknowledgement of the important role of the reference librarian. Along with this factor, the authors approach the use of media with the recognition of the validity of several concurrent methods, old and new, of handling a reference situation. One article illustrates how media and reference have been historically intertwined with the use of films, radio, television, filmstrips, audiocassettes, and videotapes. Another discusses the challenges of cataloging and/or archiving Internet and digital material. The importance of LOEX (Library Orientation Exchange) in its role of encouraging innovations in using media in reference and bibliographic instruction situations was discussed. These newer technologies have raised challenges that involve funding the costs of constantly evolving media and hardware; and dealing with lack of technical expertise to maintain equipment as reference staff are stretched further and fatigue sets in. Higher expectations of users, licensing and technical standardization issues arise.

Despite the obstacles, authors outline creative ways to obtain grant money through the dovetailing of library proposals with those of other units on a campus or of agencies off campus. Library institutions thought of as stodgy are partnering with state agencies to develop statewide networks. Because they have long gone together, reference and instruction are both benefiting greatly from the development of newer types of media, particularly such technologies as CU-SeeMe from Cornell which has fostered communication of distance learners with librarians. This dual mission of libraries is shown to benefit from and be challenged by new media. The emphasis on critical thinking and adaptable skills is stressed over learning physical locations or idiosyncratic searching methods. No author adopted a hortatory stance trying to convince librarians that they should rapidly adopt technologies, rather their general position was the partnership of humans and technology in solving information needs.

Mary Ellen Collins, PhD
Associate Professor of Library Science
Education Bibliographer/
Reference Librarian
Purdue University

Reference Services and Media

Reference Services and Media has been co-published simultaneously as *The Reference Librarian*, Number 65 1999.

The *Reference Librarian* Monographic "Separates"

Below is a list of "separates," which in serials librarianship means a special issue simultaneously published as a special journal issue or double-issue *and* as a "separate" hardbound monograph. (This is a format which we also call a "DocuSerial.")

"Separates" are published because specialized libraries or professionals may wish to purchase a specific thematic issue by itself in a format which can be separately cataloged and shelved, as opposed to purchasing the journal on an on-going basis. Faculty members may also more easily consider a "separate" for classroom adoption.

"Separates" are carefully classified separately with the major book jobbers so that the journal tie-in can be noted on new book order slips to avoid duplicate purchasing.

You may wish to visit Haworth's website at . . .

http://www.haworthpressinc.com

. . . to search our online catalog for complete tables of contents of these separates and related publications.

You may also call 1-800-HAWORTH (outside US/Canada: 607-722-5857), or Fax 1-800-895-0582 (outside US/Canada: 607-771-0012), or e-mail at:

getinfo@haworthpressinc.com

Reference Services and Media, edited by Martha Merrill, PhD, (No. 65, 1999). *Gives you valuable information about various aspects of reference services and media, including changes, planning issues, and the use and impact of new technologies.*

Coming of Age in Reference Services: A Case History of the Washington State University Libraries, edited by Christy Zlatos, MSLS (No. 64, 1999). *A celebration of the perseverance, ingenuity, and talent of the librarians who have served, past and present, at the Holland Library reference desk.*

Document Delivery Services: Contrasting Views, edited by Robin Kinder, MLS (No. 63, 1999). *Reviews the planning and process of implementing document delivery in four university libraries–Miami University, University of Colorado at Denver, University of Montana at Missoula, and Purdue University Libraries.*

The Holocaust: Memories, Research, Reference, edited by Robert Hauptman, PhD, and Susan Hubbs Motin (No. 61/62, 1998). *"A wonderful resource for reference librarians, students, and teachers . . . on how to present this painful, historical event." (Ephraim Kaye, PhD, The International School for Holocaust Studies, Yad Vashem, Jerusalem)*

Electronic Resources: Use and User Behavior, edited by Hemalata Iyer, PhD (No. 60, 1998). *Covers electronic resources and their use in libraries, with emphasis on the Internet and the Geographic Information Systems (GIS).*

Philosophies of Reference Service, edited by Celia Hales Mabry (No. 59, 1997). *"Recommended reading for any manager responsible for managing reference services and hiring reference librarians in any type of library." (Charles R. Anderson, MLS, Associate Director for Public Services, King County Library System, Bellevue, Washington)*

Business Reference Services and Sources: How End Users and Librarians Work Together, edited by Katherine M. Shelfer (No. 58, 1997). *"This is an important collection of papers suitable for all business librarians.. . . . Highly recommended!" (Lucy Heckman, MLS, MBA, Business and Economics Reference Librarian, St. John's University, Jamaica, New York)*

Reference Sources on the Internet: Off the Shelf and onto the Web, edited by Karen R. Diaz (No. 57, 1997). *Surf off the library shelves and onto the Internet and cut your research time in half!*

Reference Services for Archives and Manuscripts, edited by Laura B. Cohen (No. 56, 1997). *"Features stimulating and interesting essays on security in archives, ethics in the archival profession, and electronic records." ("The Year's Best Professional Reading" (1998), Library Journal)*

Career Planning and Job Searching in the Information Age, edited by Elizabeth A. Lorenzen, MLS (No. 55, 1996). *"Offers stimulating background for dealing with the issues of technology and service. . . . A reference tool to be looked at often." (The One-Person Library)*

The Roles of Reference Librarians: Today and Tomorrow, edited by Kathleen Low, MLS (No. 54, 1996). *"A great asset to all reference collections. . . . Presents important, valuable information for reference librarians as well as other library users." (Library Times International)*

Reference Services for the Unserved, edited by Fay Zipkowitz, MSLS, DA (No. 53, 1996). *"A useful tool in developing strategies to provide services to all patrons." (Science Books & Films)*

Library Instruction Revisited: Bibliographic Instruction Comes of Age, edited by Lyn Elizabeth M. Martin, MLS (No. 51/52, 1995). *"A powerful collection authored by respected practitioners who have stormed the bibliographic instruction (BI) trenches and, luckily for us, have recounted their successes and shortcomings." (The Journal of Academic Librarianship)*

Library Users and Reference Services, edited by Jo Bell Whitlatch, PhD (No. 49/50, 1995). *"Well-planned, balanced, and informative. . . . Both new and seasoned professionals will find material for service attitude formation and practical advice for the front lines of service." (Anna M. Donnelly, MS, MA, Associate Professor and Reference Librarian, St. John's University Library)*

Social Science Reference Services, edited by Pam Baxter, MLS (No. 48, 1995). *"Offers practical guidance to the reference librarian. . . . a valuable source of information about specific literatures within the social sciences and the skills and techniques needed to provide access to those literatures." (Nancy P. O'Brien, MLS, Head, Education and Social Science Library, and Professor of Library Administration, University of Illinois at Urbana-Champaign)*

Reference Services in the Humanities, edited by Judy Reynolds, MLS (No. 47, 1994). *"A well-chosen collection of situations and challenges encountered by reference librarians in the humanities." (College Research Library News)*

Racial and Ethnic Diversity in Academic Libraries: Multicultural Issues, edited by Deborah A. Curry, MLS, MA, Susan Griswold Blandy, MEd, and Lyn Elizabeth M. Martin, MLS (No. 45/46, 1994). *"The useful techniques and attractive strategies presented here will provide the incentive for fellow professionals in academic libraries around the country to go and do likewise in their own institutions." (David Cohen, Adjunct Professor of Library Science, School of Library and Information Science, Queens College; Director, EMIE (Ethnic Materials Information Exchange); Editor, EMIE Bulletin)*

School Library Reference Services in the 90s: Where We Are, Where We're Heading, edited by Carol Truett, PhD (No. 44, 1994). *"Unique and valuable to the the teacher-librarian as well as students of librarianship. . . . The overall work successfully interweaves the concept of the continuously changing role of the teacher-librarian." (Emergency Librarian)*

Reference Services Planning in the 90s, edited by Gail Z. Eckwright, MLS, and Lori M. Keenan, MLS (No. 43, 1994.) *"This monograph is well-researched and definitive, encompassing reference service as practices by library and information scientists. . . . it should be required reading for all professional librarian trainees." (Féliciter)*

Librarians on the Internet: Impact on Reference Services, edited by Robin Kinder, MLS (No. 41/42, 1994). *"Succeeds in demonstrating that the Internet is becoming increasingly a challenging but practical and manageable tool in the reference librarian's ever-expanding armory." (Reference Reviews)*

Reference Service Expertise, edited by Bill Katz (No. 40, 1993). *This important volume presents a wealth of practical ideas for improving the art of reference librarianship.*

Modern Library Technology and Reference Services, edited by Samuel T. Huang, MLS, MS (No. 39, 1993). *"This book packs a surprising amount of information into a relatively few number of pages. . . . This book will answer many questions." (Science Books and Films)*

Assessment and Accountability in Reference Work, edited by Susan Griswold Blandy, Lyn M. Martin, and Mary L. Strife (No. 38, 1992). *"An important collection of well-written, real-world chapters addressing the central questions that surround performance and services in all libraries." (Library Times International)*

The Reference Librarian and Implications of Mediation, edited by M. Keith Ewing, MLS, and Robert Hauptman, MLS (No. 37, 1992). *"An excellent and thorough analysis of reference mediation. . . . well worth reading by anyone involved in the delivery of reference services." (Fred Batt, MLS, Associate University Librarian for Public Services, California State University, Sacramento)*

Library Services for Career Planning, Job Searching and Employment Opportunities, edited by Byron Anderson, MA, MLS (No. 36, 1992). *"An interesting book which tells professional libraries how to set up career information centers. . . . Clearly valuable reading for anyone establishing a career library." (Career Opportunities News)*

In the Spirit of 1992: Access to Western European Libraries and Literature, edited by Mary M. Huston, PhD, and Maureen Pastine, MLS (No. 35, 1992). *"A valuable and practical [collection] which every subject specialist in the field would do well to consult." (Western European Specialists Section Newsletter)*

Access Services: The Convergence of Reference and Technical Services, edited by Gillian M. McCombs, ALA (No. 34, 1992). *"Deserves a wide readership among both technical and public services librarians. . . . highly recommended for any librarian interested in how reference and technical services roles may be combined." (Library Resources & Technical Services)*

Opportunities for Reference Services: The Bright Side of Reference Services in the 1990s, edited by Bill Katz (No. 33, 1991). *"A well-deserved look at the brighter side of reference services. . . . Should be read by reference librarians and their administrators in all types of libraries." (Library Times International)*

Government Documents and Reference Services, edited by Robin Kinder, MLS (No. 32, 1991). *Discusses access possibilities and policies with regard to government information, covering such important topics as new and impending legislation, information on most frequently used and requested sources, and grant writing.*

The Reference Library User: Problems and Solutions, edited by Bill Katz (No. 31, 1991). *"Valuable information and tangible suggestions that will help us as a profession look critically at our users and decide how they are best served." (Information Technology and Libraries)*

Continuing Education of Reference Librarians, edited by Bill Katz (No. 30/31, 1990). *"Has something for everyone interested in this field. . . . Library trainers and library school teachers may well find stimulus in some of the programs outlined here." (Library Association Record)*

Weeding and Maintenance of Reference Collections, edited by Sydney J. Pierce, PhD, MLS (No. 29, 1990). *"This volume may spur you on to planned activity before lack of space dictates 'ad hoc' solutions." (New Library World)*

Serials and Reference Services, edited by Robin Kinder, MLS, and Bill Katz (No. 27/28, 1990). *"The concerns and problems discussed are those of serials and reference librarians everywhere. . . . The writing is of a high standard and the book is useful and entertaining. . . . This book can be recommended." (Library Association Record)*

Rothstein on Reference: . . . with some help from friends, edited by Bill Katz and Charles Bunge, PhD, MLS (No. 25/26, 1990). *"An important and stimulating collection of essays on reference librarianship. . . . Highly recommended!" (Richard W. Grefrath, MA, MLS, Reference Librarian, University of Nevada Library)* Dedicated to the work of Sam Rothstein, one of the world's most respected teachers of reference librarians, this special volume features his writings as well as articles written about him and his teachings by other professionals in the field.

Integrating Library Use Skills Into the General Education Curriculum, edited by Maureen Pastine, MLS, and Bill Katz (No. 24, 1989). *"All contributions are written and presented to a high standard with excellent references at the end of each. . . . One of the best summaries I have seen on this topic." (Australian Library Review)*

Expert Systems in Reference Services, edited by Christine Roysdon, MLS, and Howard D. White, PhD, MLS (No. 23, 1989). *"The single most comprehensive work on the subject of expert systems in reference service." (Information Processing and Management)*

Information Brokers and Reference Services, edited by Bill Katz, and Robin Kinder, MLS (No. 22, 1989). *"An excellent tool for reference librarians and indispensable for anyone seriously considering their own information-brokering service." (Booklist)*

Information and Referral in Reference Services, edited by Marcia Stucklen Middleton, MLS and Bill Katz (No. 21, 1988). *Investigates a wide variety of situations and models which fall under the umbrella of information and referral.*

Reference Services and Public Policy, edited by Richard Irving, MLS, and Bill Katz (No. 20, 1988). *Looks at the relationship between public policy and information and reports ways in which libraries respond to the need for public policy information.*

Finance, Budget, and Management for Reference Services, edited by Ruth A. Fraley, MLS, MBA, and Bill Katz (No. 19, 1989). *"Interesting and relevant to the current state of financial needs in reference service. . . . A must for anyone new to or already working in the reference service area." (Riverina Library Review)*

Current Trends in Information: Research and Theory, edited by Bill Katz, and Robin Kinder, MLS (No. 18, 1984.) *"Practical direction to improve reference services and does so in a variety of ways ranging from humorous and clever metaphoric comparisons to systematic and practical methodological descriptions." (American Reference Books Annual)*

International Aspects of Reference and Information Services, edited by Bill Katz, and Ruth A. Fraley, MLS, MBA (No. 17, 1987). *"An informative collection of essays written by eminent librarians, library school staff, and others concerned with the international aspects of information work." (Library Association Record)*

Reference Services Today: From Interview to Burnout, edited by Bill Katz, and Ruth A. Fraley, MLS, MBA (No. 16, 1987). *Authorities present important advice to all reference librarians on the improvement of service and the enhancement of the public image of reference services.*

The Publishing and Review of Reference Sources, edited by Bill Katz, and Robin Kinder, MLS (No. 15, 1987). *"A good review of current reference reviewing and publishing trends in the United States . . . will be of interest to intending reviewers, reference librarians, and students." (Australasian College Libraries)*

Personnel Issues in Reference Services, edited by Bill Katz, and Ruth Fraley, MLS, MBA (No. 14, 1986). *"Chock-full of information that can be applied to most reference settings. Recommended for libraries with active reference departments." (RQ)*

Reference Services in Archives, edited by Lucille Whalen (No. 13, 1986). *"Valuable for the insights it provides on the reference process in archives and as a source of information on the different ways of carrying out that process." (Library and Information Science Annual)*

Conflicts in Reference Services, edited by Bill Katz, and Ruth A. Fraley, MLS, MBA (No. 12, 1985). *This collection examines issues pertinent to the reference department.*

Evaluation of Reference Services, edited by Bill Katz, and Ruth A. Fraley, MLS, MBA (No. 11, 1985). *"A much-needed overview of the present state of the art vis-à-vis reference service evaluation. . . . excellent. . . . Will appeal to reference professionals and aspiring students." (RQ)*

Library Instruction and Reference Services, edited by Bill Katz, and Ruth A. Fraley, MLS, MBA (No. 10, 1984). *"Well written, clear, and exciting to read. This is an important work recommended for all librarians, particularly those involved in, interested in, or considering bibliographic instruction. . . . A milestone in library literature." (RQ)*

Reference Services and Technical Services: Interactions in Library Practice, edited by Gordon Stevenson and Sally Stevenson (No. 9, 1984). *"New ideas and longstanding problems are handled with humor and sensitivity as practical suggestions and new perspectives are suggested by the authors." (Information Retrieval & Library Automation)*

Reference Services for Children and Young Adults, edited by Bill Katz, and Ruth A. Fraley, MLS, MBA (No. 7/8, 1983). *"Offers a well-balanced approach to reference service for children and young adults. " (RQ)*

Video to Online: Reference Services in the New Technology, edited by Bill Katz, and Ruth A. Fraley, MLS, MBA (No. 5/6, 1983). *"A good reference manual to have on hand. . . . well-written, concise, provide[s] a wealth of information." (Online)*

Ethics and Reference Services, edited by Bill Katz, and Ruth A. Fraley, MLS, MBA (No. 4, 1982). *Library experts discuss the major ethical and legal impications that reference librarians must take into consideration when handling sensitive inquiries about confidential material.*

Reference Services Administration and Management, edited by Bill Katz and Ruth A. Fraley, MLS, MBA (No. 3, 1982). *Librarianship experts discuss the management of the reference function in libraries and information centers, outlining the responsibilities and qualifications of reference heads.*

Reference Services in the 1980s, edited by Bill Katz (No. 1/2, 1982). *Here is a thought-provoking volume on the future of reference services in libraries, with an emphasis on the challenges and needs that have come about as a result of automation.*

Reference Services and Media

Martha Merrill
Editor

Reference Services and Media has been co-published
simultaneously as *The Reference Librarian*, Number 65 1999.

The Haworth Information Press
An Imprint of
The Haworth Press, Inc.
New York • London • Oxford

Published by

The Haworth Information Press, 10 Alice Street, Binghamton, NY 13904-1580, USA

The Haworth Press Information Press, is an imprint of The Haworth Press, Inc., 10 Alice Street, Binghamton, NY 13904-1580 USA.

Reference Services and Media has been co-published simultaneously as *The Reference Librarian*, Number 65 1999.

The development, preparation, and publication of this work has been undertaken with great care. However, the publisher, employees, editors, and agents of The Haworth Press and all imprints of The Haworth Press, Inc., including The Haworth Medical Press® and Pharmaceutical Products Press®, are not responsible for any errors contained herein or for consequences that may ensue from use of materials or information contained in this work. Opinions expressed by the author(s) are not necessarily those of The Haworth Press, Inc.

Cover design by Thomas J. Mayshock Jr.

Library of Congress Cataloging-in-Publication Data

Reference services and media/Martha Merrill, editor.
     p. cm.
     "Co-published simultaneously as The Reference librarian, number 65, 1999."
     Includes bibliographical references and index.
     ISBN 0-7890-0695-2 (acid-free paper)
     1. Reference services (Libraries–United States. 2. Multimedia library services–United States. 3. Academic libraries–Reference systems. I. Merrill, Martha.
Z711.R44923 1999
025.5'2–dc21
                                                 99-30029
                                                 CIP

INDEXING & ABSTRACTING

Contributions to this publication are selectively indexed or abstracted in print, electronic, online, or CD-ROM version(s) of the reference tools and information services listed below. This list is current as of the copyright date of this publication. See the end of this section for additional notes.

- *Academic Abstracts/CD-ROM*

- *Academic Search: data base of 2,000 selected academic serials, updated monthly*

- *BUBL Information Service: An Internet-Based Information Service for the UK Higher Education Community*

- *CNPIEC Reference Guide: Chinese National Directory of Foreign Periodicals*

- *Current Awareness Abstracts of Library & Information Management literature, ASLUB (UK)*

- *Current Index to Journals in Education*

- *Educational Administration Abstracts (EAA)*

- *IBZ International Bibliography of Periodical Literature*

- *Index to Periodical Articles Related to Law*

- *Information Science Abstracts*

- *Informed Librarian, The*

- *INSPEC*

- *Journal of Academic Librarianship: Guide to Professional Literature, The*

- *Konyvtari Figyelo-Library Review*

(continued)

- *Library & Information Science Abstracts (LISA)*

- *Library and Information Science Annual (LISCA)*

- *Library Literature*

- *MasterFILE: updated database from EBSCO Publishing*

- *Newsletter of Library and Information Services*

- *OT BibSys*

- *Referativnyi Zhurnal (Abstracts Journal of the All-Russian Institute of Scientific and Technical Information)*

- *Sage Public Administration Abstracts (SPAA)*

Special Bibliographic Notes related to special journal issues (separates) and indexing/abstracting

- indexing/abstracting services in this list will also cover material in any "separate" that is co-published simultaneously with Haworth's special thematic journal issue or DocuSerial. Indexing/abstracting usually covers material at the article/chapter level.
- monographic co-editions are intended for either non-subscribers or libraries which intend to purchase a second copy for their circulating collections.
- monographic co-editions are reported to all jobbers/wholesalers/approval plans. The source journal is listed as the "series" to assist the prevention of duplicate purchasing in the same manner utilized for books-in-series.
- to facilitate user/access services all indexing/abstracting services are encouraged to utilize the co-indexing entry note indicated at the bottom of the first page of each article/chapter/contribution.
- this is intended to assist a library user of any reference tool (whether print, electronic, online, or CD-ROM) to locate the monographic version if the library has purchased this version but not a subscription to the source journal.
- individual articles/chapters in any Haworth publication are also available through the Haworth Document Delivery Service (HDDS).

Reference Services
and Media

CONTENTS

ABOUT THE EDITOR

Martha Merrill, PhD, is Professor of Instructional Media at Jacksonville State University in Jacksonville, AL, where she teaches in the graduate level school library media program. She received her doctorate in library science from the University of Pittsburgh. The author of articles for *Library Journal, The High School Magazine, Southeastern Librarian*, and the *Alabama Librarian*, she is a co-author of a book to be published by Libraries Unlimited. She has chaired and served on committees at the national, regional, and state levels as well as served as president of the Alabama Library Association. Dr. Merrill's honors include the Alabama/SIRS Intellectual Freedom Award, the Alabama Library Association Distinguished Service Award, and the Alabama Beta Phi Mu Librarian of the Year Award.

Introduction

Technology continues to change the format of reference materials and the function of reference services. This volume is an eclectic one covering different aspects of reference services and media. Aspects such as overviews of changes, planning issues, and use and impact of new technologies are discussed. The focus includes articles related to academic and public libraries. I wish to thank those who contributed to this volume for sharing their research, their ideas, and their professional experiences. It is hoped that these articles will provide information on and reflection about the issues relating to the incorporation of media in reference services.

Martha Merrill

[Haworth co-indexing entry note]: "Introduction." Merrill, Martha. Co-published simultaneously in *The Reference Librarian* (The Haworth Information Press, an imprint of the Haworth Press, Inc.) No. 65, 1999, p. 1; and: *Reference Services and Media* (ed: Martha Merrill) The Haworth Information Press, an imprint of The Haworth Press, Inc., 1999, p. 1. Single or multiple copies of this article are available for a fee from The Haworth Document Delivery Service [1-800-342-9678, 9:00 a.m. - 5:00 p.m. (EST). E-mail address: getinfo@haworthpressinc.com].

1

MEDIA ISSUES

Information Services
in the Year 2000 and Beyond

T. Harmon Straiton, Jr.

SUMMARY. Today's libraries–academic, research, public, and elementary and secondary schools–are in the midst of an extended period of unprecedented change and adjustment. Having never been static organizations, they have existed within and responded to changes in the communities they exist to serve. Computerization, electronics, and telecommunications have resulted in the alteration of almost every function performed in libraries today. The reference services extended by these libraries are no different. In keeping with their missions and goals, they must adopt and incorporate the new information technology now as well as the year 2000 and beyond. Problems and challenges which must be solved and met are discussed. There is no doubt that the library user will benefit as services are expanded to include among other innovations: services expanded beyond the walls of the library and its physical collection, interactive face-to-face teleconferencing with information specialists, and machines utilizing artificial intelligence which assist in identifying and locating information. *[Article copies available for a fee from The Haworth Document Delivery Service: 1-800-342-9678. E-mail address: getinfo@haworthpressinc.com]*

T. Harmon Straiton, Jr. is Head, Microforms and Documents Department, Auburn University Libraries, Ralph Brown Draughon Library, 231 Mell St., Auburn University, AL 36849-5606.

[Haworth co-indexing entry note]: "Information Services in the Year 2000 and Beyond." Straiton, T. Harmon Jr. Co-published simultaneously in *The Reference Librarian* (The Haworth Information Press, an imprint of The Haworth Press, Inc.) No. 65, 1999, pp. 3-14; and: *Reference Services and Media* (ed: Martha Merrill) The Haworth Information Press, an imprint of The Haworth Press, Inc., 1999, pp. 3-14. Single or multiple copies of this article are available for a fee from The Haworth Document Delivery Service [1-800-342-9678, 9:00 a.m. - 5:00 p.m. (EST). E-mail address: getinfo@haworthpressinc.com].

KEYWORDS. Reference services, information technology, electronic resources

"Knowledge will forever govern ignorance and that people who mean to be their own governors must arm themselves with the power that knowledge gives. A popular government without popular information or means of acquiring it is but a prologue to a farce or tragedy or perhaps both."[1] Reference librarians as well as other information professionals have long respected these words of James Madison and continue to acknowledge the importance of his message. Nowhere could this be truer than in the provision of access to information resources.

Libraries are in the midst of a period of unprecedented change and adjustment. Having never been static organizations, they have existed within and responded to changes in the communities they exist to serve. Computerization, electronics, and telecommunications have resulted in the alteration of almost every function performed in libraries today. The reference services extended by these libraries are no different.

It used to be referred to as reference. Then it became reference and information service. Now it is information systems and technology. The changes in the terminology are a strong indication that there is an evolution occurring in the delivery of information services and that this evolution will continue at a rapid pace well into the 21st Century. In fact with the " . . . exponential growth of new and emerging technologies, these can no longer be considered simple evolutionary changes. Continual technological advances are changing public demand for goods and services worldwide, and libraries, like other institutions, appear to be grappling with how to successfully manage this change."[2]

In order to meet this information challenge, there are several considerations which have to be resolved. The litany is long and complicated and includes, but is not limited to: (a) formats and their compatibility, (b) archiving of data and bibliographic information for historical purposes, (c) the training of reference professionals and library users, (d) costs, and (e) the information haves and have nots.

"A new technology is composed of two parts: a new kind of physical device and a new philosophy or method for using it. One generally cannot be used without the other."[3] While somewhat dated, this observation is no less true in the age of changing information delivery. Information resources are being distributed in a variety of formats. There are the traditional physical formats of paper and microforms with their documented and discussed advantages and disadvantages. While some reference librarians and users still feel more comfortable with these formats, more resources are being distributed electronically only with no real physical equivalent.

There are the electronic formats including diskettes, CD-ROMs, DVDs, and the various Internet or Web-based versions. Not so long ago, the distribution of data sets in the form of diskettes was thought to be a wave of the future but technological changes brought problems. The standard size diskette or "floppy" was 5 1/4-inch square which then became the current 3 1/2-inch diskette. Although smaller in size, the second diskette could be manufactured as high density resulting in a capability of storing a great deal more data. For obvious reasons, the two are not compatible.

The Library Programs Service (LPS) of the U.S. Government Printing Office recognized this problem when it issued its minimum technical standards for a work station or PCs to be used in member libraries of the Federal Depository Library Program.[4] These standards recommended that each computer include means for using both types of diskettes. The specifications for computer equipment are to insure that the equipment is sufficient to allow timely and equitable public access to Government electronic information products.

Librarians were encouraged to ". . . consider such local factors as the amount of information provided by the government over the Internet as compared with the amount from CD-ROM, whether and how the work stations are networked, to what extent users are permitted to perform additional information processing at public access work stations, whether users are experiencing extended waiting times at the library peak service hours, etc."[5] LPS suggested that the specifications were not representative of the best possible work station rather that they are the minimum, or baseline, specifications to be considered.

In fact, what was classified as a simple basic workstation continues to become more complicated. In his discussion of electronic workstations, van Brakel[6] describes four different types: the academic workstation, the reference workstation (i.e., for library users), the information specialist workstation, and the management information workstation.

As with the dissimilar diskettes, a parallel is presently occurring in the diameter and amount of information contained on compact disks. In the not so distant past, the Data User Services Division of the U.S. Bureau of the Census broke new ground in the delivery of vast amounts of data with its *Test Disk No. 1*[7] in the format of a CD-ROM sent to selected libraries and other information agencies. The traditional CD-ROM is quickly being replaced by the digital versatile disk (DVD)–a fact not even considered several years ago.

DVD is a new optical disk technology that is expected to rapidly replace the CD-ROM disk as well as the audio compact disc over the next few years. Fortunately, most DVD players can also read CD-ROMs. The DVD holds approximately 4.7 gigabytes of information on one of its two sides, or enough for a 133-minute movie. With two layers on each of its two sides, it will hold up to 17 gigabytes of video, audio, or other information while the current CD-ROM disk of the same physical size holds only 600 megabytes. Expressed more simply, the DVD can hold more than 28 times as much information in the same amount of space. Imagine several encyclopedias and dictionaries with all the possible audio, video, text, and data files as well as the software to retrieve, display, manipulate, and even analyze all contained on a single DVD.

Remember Telnet, file transfer protocol (FTP) and GOPHER and all the benefits that reference librarians and other users derived from these computer programs and their abilities to manipulated and display data? In only the last few years, these have been replaced by the more intuitive Web and the accompanying browsers which promote the use of graphics and provide access to a wealth of knowledge as well as misinformation being mounted on this vast network of computers. Interesting enough, most Web browsers can use these same computer programs but in an almost seamless manner for the user.

"Publishers of electronic databases, however, do not usually sell their product, but instead they license it to libraries (or sites) for specific uses. They usually charge libraries a per-user fee or a per-unit fee for the specific amount of information the library uses. When libraries do not own these resources, they have less control over whether older information is saved for future use–another important cultural function of libraries. In the electronic age, questions of copyright, intellectual property rights, and the economics of information have become increasingly important to the future of library service."[8]

As there is no physical or hardcopy equivalent of the data and text contained in these various formats, it becomes even more important that the data be archived for historical and research purposes. While this preservation activity remains uneven at its best, attempts are being made to maintain and warehouse data. In the current environment, even if data are archived for later use, there is little or no true guarantee as to whether its integrity or accuracy can or will be maintained. It must be protected from censorship with its validity and reliability ensured. Federal documents librarians have been concerned as to which agency or organization will be willing to assume this daunting task. It is to be sure that similar concerns are reflected in non-Federal databases.

Meyers states in her article on reference services in a virtual library that "We've quit thinking of 'our collection.' Many computers . . . are hosts for electronic articles and preprints. Information is distributed from small computers everywhere. We find it on the Net. Our library archives material from the campus sites and many others. We cooperate with other libraries to replicate archives at multiple sites to reduce the risk of loss. Digital information is archived on discs that look very much like your CD-ROM's, but they are made of glass."[9]

Although the archiving of electronic resources has the potential of be a serious problem, the very fact that it is essential reinforces the fact that electronic resources are generally the most current or up-to-date version. This has a beneficial effect on the maintenance of reference collections and the services that they support.

As the technology changes, it will be necessary to migrate electronic resources which will involve the periodic refreshing or transfer of government information products from one medium to another in order to minimize loss of information due to physical deterioration of storage media and the reformatting of information to avoid technological obsolescence due to software or platform dependence. Some remember the punch cards used to write computer programs and to transmit data to be manipulated by those programs. In today's electronic environment, it would be difficult to find a machine that could process these individual cards. Surely the same fate should not fall to data and text simply stored in the wrong format.

The delivery of information electronically has implications both for the level of staffing at the reference desk and for the training and development of reference librarians. Staff development should include the obvious areas and some of the not so obvious (e.g., technostress). Technostress has been defined as the stress experienced by reference librarians who must constantly deal with the demands of new information and the changes they produce in the workplace.[10]

In turn, the demands of library users for access and assistance exacerbates these pressures. While standardization of searching techniques and the formatting of displayed information has made some improvements for the typical reference librarian, it still is far from being complete. The lack of standardization translates into additional training needs by reference librarians and other users.

Perhaps one of the most detrimental problems in this area is the inability or lack of desire in accepting the new technology. If reference librarians or information specialists relate to new technologies from the traditional frame of reference, the true impact of the innovation will be missed or reduced. For example, even with the capabilities of electronic mail, many libraries and their reference personnel favor the traditional walk-in patron over that of one who "ask a librarian" via library Web pages.

"The reference librarian of the future will be more closely involved with research into better ways of providing information to users–e.g., making computer systems more friendly, creating more sophisticated databases, testing new technologies, and experimenting with different approaches to information–yet the emphasis on personal contact must not be lost."[11] A more daunting and challenging technological change to affect reference services is real-time interfacing. Many Web browsers already have the capability to incorporate real-time audio, video, and data conferencing applications. As these functions are more readily accepted by users and standards are written and accepted, there is the prospect of reference librarians providing information services face to face in a teleconferencing mode with remote patrons.

In the face of decreasing enrollment or the lack of the ability to handle additional on-campus enrollment and increasing information technology, future expansion of off-campus or distance education programs is a real possibility. Remote access from those sites is essential as is this ability to conduct a reference interview in a real-time environment.

Reference services are already enjoying another benefit of electronic resources–timeliness in the delivery of the information. Gone are the days of waiting for the latest edition of a reference directory or a

Supreme Court decision announced only two hours earlier. Access via the Web results in instant user satisfaction and diminishes the time required to receive and process the hardcopy material.

Imagine using e-mail to inform reference users of the table of contents of a newly arrived hardcopy or Web-based publication. Such services exist with commercial document delivery suppliers which e-mail the table of contents of numerous journals based on user profiles to clients. The same could be true for standard reference works especially those which are electronic. Should e-mail be a problem and as a reference service, libraries could provide patron-initiated electronic access to these publications.

Campbell argues that the technical and conceptional foundations of reference librarianship must change if it is to survive the information age and proposes a new model of service, called "access engineering," in which information seekers are treated as consumers, and technology is used to route information to them on demand[12]–a proposal which a growing number of information specialists are accepting as an appropriate model for the delivery of information.

The Auburn University Libraries have designed and implemented an electronic reference service to support the university's land-grant mission. Agents of both the agricultural extension and experiment services assigned to the state's 67 counties complained of being isolated and lacking direct access to library services. An electronic reference services model was designed and implemented to address and meet these needs and demands. Access to the Libraries' OPAC, databases, and electronic indexes is easily available. A number of full-text databases allow access to journal articles. For information not yet available in full-text electronic versions, an online request form has been implemented and materials are photocopied and mailed or faxed. A logical step would be to digitize the information. The digital information could be easily e-mailed to the appropriate agent.

Even the type and quality of reference questions being asked of reference personnel is changing. As users become more sophisticated, they also become more demanding in their expectations of the reference services being provided by libraries. Reference librarians can now answer many more factual questions as a result of advances in technology. Libraries which include bibliographic instruction within these reference services are expecting a demand for more and better sessions on gaining access to electronic resources. Everything from training in using Microsoft's Windows™ software to use of Web search engines is needed and expected.

Reference librarians are not the only information specialists who are directly affected by changes in the delivery of information in electronic formats. Librarians and staff who offer and implement the technical services for libraries are also being affected dramatically. Acquisition departments are being forced to negotiate legal contracts and pricing structures for electronic resources–standalone CD-ROMs, networked CD-ROMs or LANs, and access to databases mounted on the Internet or Web.

Catalogers, both monographic and serials, now automatically or instinctively add universal resource locators (URLs) to bibliographic records which form the Web-based online public access catalogs used by a growing number of libraries. Adding such information to the standard MARC record promotes the use of the bibliographic record by library users and reference professionals as a means to speed dial access to data and text mounted on the Internet.

The technology of electronic resources assures their ability to address the needs of reference librarians and library users with an almost minute-by-minute response to these shifts. Therein lies one problem. The URLs included in such bibliographic records change without notice and for the smallest of reasons. A tremendous effort must be made to maintain the accuracy of these finding aids. In the past, as a general rule, a bibliographic record was constructed, checked for accuracy, and added to the OPAC. After this, it was seldom touched or modified except to reflect changes in titles or subject headings. Full record and table of contents searching has somewhat reduced the need for updating or changing subject headings; however, URLs require constant supervision and modification.

While there are many benefits inherent in the use of electronic information, including more timely and broader public access, there are no conclusive data at this time to support the assertion that it will result in significant savings. The costs of providing electronic access to information has to be absorbed by the library budget or additional funding resources identified and secured. Traditional patterns of library budget allocations will evolve or change so that opportunities for new or enhanced service based upon technology are established as priorities.

It is not unusual for an electronic resource to cost twice as much as its paper equivalent, and once a subscription has been acquired, the cost often exceeds inflation. In the past 20 years, the size, activity, and cost of library and other information services have grown above the growth rates of basic indexes.[13] The ease of access from within the library building and from outside the walls of the building, the ability to identify information using the traditional access points of author, title, and subject as well as keyword or phrases, and the fact that more users can access the database simultaneously often justify or outweigh the additional costs. Furthermore, additional cooperative or consortia efforts where FTEs can be lumped together for pricing purposes and structure will become the norm and not the exception. In some areas or state, this is already a fact.

Many journal or newspaper databases include the full-text of a majority of the articles indexed and abstracted and can result in the cancellation of those resources also available in the traditional formats. More libraries are opting for the cancellation of serial titles in these traditional formats with the intent of providing electronic access to the full-text of their contents.

The fact is that information retrieval and the searching capabilities that accompany it are steadily and surely shifting emphasis from the complete book or entire article to individual paragraphs and even single sentences within the book or article. Reference services are moving beyond simple bibliographic access toward actual document delivery and in doing so are accepting the responsibility for providing both information and documents. More libraries are choosing to provide a mixture of traditional, full-text electronic resources and actual document delivery via a commercial document supplier or vendor at little or no value-added cost to the library users.

While remote users can often access library bibliographic and data files, they may lack the necessary computer equipment and peripherals or the expertise to effectively and efficiently identify and retrieve the desired information. While reference librarians cannot resolve the problem of the lack of appropriate computer equipment by a remote user, they can maintain the necessary equipment within the library. In addition, reference librarians can offer advice and consent with appropriate reference strategies in using electronic resources.

Without the intervention of reference librarians and libraries, will we become a nation of information have's and have not's? Nancy Kranich stated that "Government information is of inestimable value to the American public. Assuring the public's right to this information requires a democratic caretaker no smaller than the government itself. No other entity can assume the primary responsibility for collecting, organizing, and disseminating the public's information assets, nor guarantee the public's equal rights to use and repackage it."[14] Surely libraries have some obligation in providing free or inexpensive access to electronic resources.

As the Internet began as a means of the government and research institutions sharing data and information, and expanded beyond that rather limited scope, academic libraries and their parent institutions have often been the leaders in providing access to electronic resources useful in the provision of reference and information services to library users. Using grants and donations from corporations and individuals, public libraries are making a concerted effort to enhance their access services to include the information super highway with fewer restrictions placed on its availability. Elementary and secondary schools are slowly incorporating electronic resources into classrooms and libraries.

A few years ago, forecasters predicted the virtual disappearance of libraries as electronic communication led to a paperless society. Libraries and their reference services neither disappeared nor became paperless. Traditional library materials and electronic resources will continue to coexist.[15]

Librarians–be they referred to as reference librarians, information specialists, information scientists, or cybrarians–will find that libraries and reference services will experience a combination of different degrees of virtuality:

> *Level 1:* electronic access (OPAC [Online Public Access Catalog]) but real library in the background. This corresponds to the first phase of library automation.
> *Level 2:* electronic access to virtual collections but with delivery of real documents (i.e., UNCOVER).
> *Level 3:* electronic access to virtual collections consisting of electronic documents.[16]

Despite the lack of any long-term, sustained successes in the area of such systems, it is possible that future electronic reference services will utilize expert systems for the purposes of enhancing or supplementing reference services. Expert systems are knowledge-based computer programs which represent a branch of the study of artificial intelligence. Goodall has defined an expert system as "a computer system that uses a representation of human expertise in a specialist domain in order to perform functions similar to those normally performed by a human expert in that domain."[17] "The majority of reference expert systems are doomed to failure because they try to suggest particular reference works. As the number of reference works increases, so does the difficulty in implementing and maintaining the expert system."[18]

In contrast, as a librarian conducts the reference interview, there is an immediate and ongoing interaction with the library user. Qualities reflecting the information needs of the individual are assembled and used to identify one or more works which would prove useful in answering the question. Of course, the same technique can be employed by computers to supplement reference service. After the question-and answer period, the system could construct search strategies to be applied against a database(s) of information–OPACs of traditional library materials and bibliographic databases hosted by commercial or government suppliers (i.e., DIALOG or MEDLARS) or a number of Web-based resources or search engines.

Even so, it will never be possible to meet all reference needs with computer-based systems, and that should not be a desirable goal, but just as the library catalog jogs our memory of the library collection, computer-based systems can become an important component of electronic reference service.

A preoccupation with technical issues misses the point as reference librarians must address whether technology is influencing information-seeking behavior of information providers. Reference departments which do not provide information access service providers and construct artificial boundaries that limit the extent of reference librarians involvement in providing information will find that there is little or no room for continued development.

The year 2000 and beyond is upon us. Emerging technologies afford tremendous opportunities for reference librarians and for improved and enhanced public access to information. These opportunities bring new challenges that require the reevaluation of access services and current information dissemination programs to take advantage of new opportunities with a minimum of disruption of quality reference services during this period of rapid technological change.

REFERENCES

1. Madison, James. "Letter to W. T. Barry, August 4, 1882." in Hunt, Gaillard, ed. *The Writings of James Madison.* New York: Bantam, 1910. Vol. IX: 103.

2. Pitkin, Gary M., ed. 1995. *The Impact of Emerging Technologies on Reference Service and Bibliographic Instruction.* Westport, Conn.: Greenwood Press, p. 25.

3. Mooers, C.N. 1976. "The management of Information Handling–A Pioneer's View." *Bulletin of the American Society for Information Science* 2(8): 18-21.

4. U.S. Superintendent of Documents. May 15, 1996. "Recommended Minimum Specifications for Public Access Work Stations in Federal Depository Libraries." *Administrative Notes* 17(07): 1.

5. U.S. Superintendent of Documents. May 15, 1996. "Recommended Minimum Specifications for Public Access Work Stations in Federal Depository Libraries." *Administrative Notes* 17(07): 2.

6. van Brakel, Pieter A. Aug.-Oct. 1991. "The Electronic Workstation: Challenges for the Information Specialist." *Electronic Library* 9(4-5): 211-15.

7. U.S. Bureau of the Census. Data User Services Division. [1990?] *Test Disk No. 1.* [Washington]: Reference Technology, Inc.

8. "Libraries: The Changing Role of Libraries." *Britannica Online.* http://www.eb.com:180/cgi-bin/g?DocF=marco/5003/74/0.html [Accessed 04 March 1998].

9. Meyers, Judy E. 1997. "Reference Services in the Virtual Library." In Ensor, Pat, ed. *The Cybrarian's Manual.* Chicago and London: American Library Association, p. 423.

10. Kupersmith, John. 1992. "Technostress and the Reference Librarian." *RSR: Reference Services Review* 20(2): 7-14, 50.

11. Dunstan, Peter. 1986. *Librarianship: The Challenge of the Information and Electronic Revolution.* [ERIC ED 277 373].

12. Campbell, Jerry D. 1992. "Shaking the Conceptional Foundations of Reference: A Perspective." *RSR: Reference Services Review* 20(4): 29-36.

13. Oettinger, Anthony G. *Elements of Information Resources Policy: Library and Other Information Services.* Cambridge, Mass.: Harvard University. [ERIC ED 118 067].

14. Kranich, Nancy. "The Public's Right to Know and Electronic Government Information" in Reynolds, Dennis J., ed. *Citizen Rights and Access to Electronic Information: The 1991 LITA President's Program Presentation and Background Papers.* Chicago, Ill.: American Library Association, 1992.

15. De Gennaro, Richard. June 1982. "Libraries, Technology, and the Information Marketplace." *Library Journal* 107: 1045-54.

16. Bauwens, Michel. What is Cyberspace? in Ensor, Pat, ed. *The Cybrarian's Manual.* Chicago and London: American Library Association, p. 398.

17. Morgan, Eric Lease. 1997. "Clarence Meets Alcuin or, Expert Systems are Still an Option in Reference Work" in Ensor, Pat, ed. *The Cybrarian's Manual.* Chicago and London: American Library Association, p. 128.

18. Ibid. p. 131.

Promise, Perils, and Planning: An Administrative Commentary on the Use of Technology to Expand Reference Services

Nancy Allen

SUMMARY. The promising future of new and better information services supported by the use of information technologies is well documented. Many journal articles describe successful experiences with better reference and instructional services, new services to new kinds of students who are engaged in distant independent learning or other non-traditional education, and better communication with library users. However, there are many perils on the way to delivering such improvements with the use of new finding tools, new software, new printing systems, and new telecommunication networks. An administrative overview of the sorts of planning which can smooth the implementation of information technology-based reference and instructional services outlines options for staffing, troubleshooting, fund raising, and budget development. Planning takes time and effort, collaboration and creativity. With appropriate emphasis on planning, the promise of implementing improvements in quality of services through information technologies can and should become a reality. *[Article copies available for a fee from The Haworth Document Delivery Service: 1-800-342-9678. E-mail address: getinfo@haworthpressinc.com]*

KEYWORDS. Reference services, information technology, digital resources, planning

Nancy Allen is Dean and Director, Penrose Library, University of Denver, 2150 E. Evans Ave., Denver, CO 80208-2007.

[Haworth co-indexing entry note]: "Promise, Perils, and Planning: An Administrative Commentary on the Use of Technology to Expand Reference Services." Allen, Nancy. Co-published simultaneously in *The Reference Librarian* (The Haworth Information Press, an imprint of The Haworth Press, Inc.) No. 65, 1999, pp. 15-28; and: *Reference Services and Media* (ed: Martha Merrill) The Haworth Information Press, an imprint of The Haworth Press, Inc., 1999, pp. 15-28. Single or multiple copies of this article are available for a fee from The Haworth Document Delivery Service [1-800-342-9678, 9:00 a.m. - 5:00 p.m. (EST). E-mail address: getinfo@haworthpressinc.com].

15

PROMISE

There is much talk about the virtual university. A recent report from a Joint Education/IBM Roundtable summarizes many of the issues involved with the higher education effort to satisfy demands of learners interested in a model based on telecommunications technologies which enable asynchronous teaching and learning, at any time, from any place.[1] While colleges and universities, and collaborative efforts such as the Western Governor's University <http://www.westgov.org/smart/vu/vu.html> and the California Virtual University <http://www.california.edu> are working to deliver quality educational programs in new ways, libraries have been working to deliver information services in new ways. Multi-type and academic library consortia and their member libraries are developing virtual collections, using a fairly recognizable definition of scope, across the United States and Canada. It is quite clear that technological tools are changing the options available for reference librarians who want to deliver information services to off-campus students, and to traditional students visiting the library as well.

There are dozens of projects described in the reference literature, and each demonstrates experimentation with new technology-based strategies for general or introductory bibliographic instruction; for advanced, subject-intensive resource management; and for the teaching of database searching or computer-based information retrieval skills. Electronic mail has completely changed the nature of communication among library staff, and at the same time, many libraries offer some way to deposit reference queries via email. In this way, electronic communication changes the picture for library public relations, for collection development feedback, for collaboration on instructional design with faculty outside the library, and more.

Finding tools are increasingly web-based. While interface and command keys continue to be confusing to library users,[2] necessitating different kinds of library-based instructional programs, more and more citation indexes are available to remote users. Many online catalogs have web interfaces and links to resources not owned or even licensed by the library. An increasing percentage of the collection budget in all types of libraries is now dedicated to digital resources in the form of CD-ROMs or site licenses, with a recent survey indicating that about 6% of the average Association of Research Libraries member's budget is committed in this way.[3] Public libraries are also focusing on digital resources, website development, and other programs to assist library users with information access. The ability of a public library user to connect to online resources made available by his or her library or library consortium can support community economic development, small business growth, individual study, and literacy. This ability certainly can produce greater workplace and personal efficiency for users of any kind of library.

These developments carry tremendous promise for enhanced quality of reference service. Outreach to information seekers who do not regularly visit a library can produce a whole new "market" of library users. Librarians have a new toolkit with which to teach information management and research strategies. Communication media are faster and more convenient for library users. New media promise rapid turnaround in research services, research assistance, document delivery, and interlibrary loan. Librarians carrying collection development responsibility can more conveniently fit in user and faculty communication among other communication needs such as liaison with teaching faculty on instructional program requests.[4]

Entrepreneurial colleges and universities are mining entirely new markets for adults who work full time but who are interested in advanced degrees or shorter forms of continued education. Bibliographic instruction, therefore, is evolving because of changes in the characteristics of students. Libraries can respond with web-based teaching, remote access to finding tools, site licenses for full-text resources and distant-independent electronic communication in order to provide library resources to adult learners. Obviously, many on-campus, traditional undergraduate and graduate students find these services convenient as well. A connection to the library's web site from a residence hall, workplace, student center cafeteria, or classroom means students can search for collection information, check citations, or write an analytical literary paper anywhere they can plug in a laptop. What is often regarded as distance education technology is soon indispensable for residential members of the university community.

In addition to the direct benefits of reference and information services technologies in higher education, there are organizational benefits. These include stronger partnerships with academic units, development of more finely tuned communication and team work skills, new capabilities to teach critical thinking and informed judgment, new ways to convey the attitude that life long learning is part of the knowledge workplace, improved student productivity, and library involvement in curricular development.[5]

PROBLEMS

Although greater visibility for the library and more effective information services may seem an easy step away from traditional paper-based reference services and collection development, a great deal of planning is needed to avoid implementation problems. To those who read the issues of *The Reference Librarian*, or *RQ* (now *Reference and User Services Quarterly*) or *Research Strategies*, the question, "What problems?" might be asked. Most articles boast of success stories, and minimize accounts of anguish, terrible morale, downed systems, printing problems, and other aspects of frustration with technology.

Over the past 25 years, most librarians, regardless of the type of information environment in which they work, have experienced technostress. The need for constant, daily re-education reduces the feeling of confidence needed by reference librarians in order to feel good about the services they provide. While Mendelsohn[6] did not mention technology as a factor producing either quality or lack thereof in her study on quality factors, it certainly is a major factor in morale and job satisfaction for experienced reference librarians. A common complaint heard by library administrators goes something like this: "I did not become a reference librarian in order to spend half my time at the desk with a paper clip un-jamming the dot matrix printers." When the printer does not work at all, the refrain is, "technology is creating yet another barrier to effective research patterns on the part of our students." When the integrated library system crashes, there may even be a bit of longing for those good old card catalog days as librarians struggle to deliver answers to the queue of students lined up while the reference librarians connect to OCLC in order to try to determine local holdings. And when the entire network, complete with telecommunications, goes down, staff can accomplish almost nothing on their job descriptions. While each problem may be a 1% problem (it works 99% of the time), a lot of different 1% problems can create quite a bit of frustration on the part of librarians and library users. The vision of transparent technology-based teaching media (such as compressed video or teleconferencing) is still usually a futuristic vision, with teleconferencing participants very much concerned about reliability of equipment and very much in need of on-site technical support.[7] (As an aside, one should note that teachers echo these concerns when they use laptops, software, email, and other academic technology tools in the classroom.)

A million things can go wrong with our promising new technology tools. And a million things will go wrong. Just as the reference librarian learns to troubleshoot the more common system maladies, new problems pop up. Each new release of interface software from vendors introduce difficulties which were not there yesterday. Each time a web browser is upgraded, a connection to a licensed resource might not work. There is probably not enough time in the week to methodically test each new release or each new software product prior to introducing these to library users, and so "live" testing is a common pattern found in libraries everywhere. All the problems are not in the library, of course. Consortial decisions on new digital resources may not match all local priorities. And if online databases are made available through servers based at consortium headquarters, technical problems there can cause access failures. At the university level, disaster strikes when the "name server" crashes, so no computer can find another computer to talk to. The roles of information professionals are quickly evolving to include network troubleshooting, microcomputer and peripheral equipment repair, telecommunications diagnosis, and other necessities of modern life in a library.

While this can feel pretty awful to the dedicated reference librarian who truly wants to deliver high quality, accurate, and responsive information services, librarians do realize the promise of new technologies. They can see, during the 99% of the time that networked resources and the systems supporting them work, that it is worth the trouble to move ahead with new services and new tools. In fact, teams of librarians, working in tandem with library administrators, can make it much more probable that technology assisted information services will work effectively.

PLANNING

While there are no universal ways to avoid the pitfalls related to information technologies used in reference and instructional services, there are some considerations that might help.

Consortia

Fewer libraries, large or small, are working to develop digital libraries independently of partnerships with other libraries through consortia. These consortia take several different forms. For small public libraries, the consortia may be a regional library service center (or region of cooperation) or a multi-type library consortium, including those based on the regional OCLC service centers. For academic libraries, groups based on partnerships arising from athletic competition have formed as have statewide alliances, regional alliances, or groups of similar institutions. Among the many benefits offered by consortia, the ability to bargain effectively and to make economies of scale available to members rises to the top. When negotiating for access to web-based resources, sharing a large pool of simultaneous users results in fewer busy signals than does contracting for an independent and usually minimal number of simultaneous users for a library's site license. Consortial pricing is usually an advantage, and more of the collection development or electronic resource budget is available for other products or publications. When consortia are hosting servers, providing authentication services, or delivering technical support, the procedures for reporting trouble must be perfectly clear to all information service staff, and the consortium should be providing seven day by twenty four hour support when libraries require it. Consortial technical support can help at the local level when the library system's office is overextended.

Reference librarians should plan for a regularized method of providing input on the selection of digital resources to be licensed by the consortium. There may be a digital library development committee, or there may be a feedback system from local libraries to the consortium. Reference librarians should find a way to communicate through the library dean or director to the consortium so that effective communication of priorities and library decisions on optional resources can be achieved. When information products or services are made available on a trial basis, reference librarians must work out a way to take advantage of these opportunities to analyze new options and to get feedback from primary stakeholders in the user community. Internal planning within each local library's reference or collection management department is time consuming, but once a system is put in place for product review and communication with library administrators and consortia, decision making should flow more smoothly, with better results for library users at a better price.

Technology Budget Development

This is an extraordinarily complex area of planning, and it is often one where reference librarians are not directly involved or even informed about the challenges or opportunities. A lack of understanding about budgetary aspects of reference and information services technologies can lead to a debilitating lack of trust in administrators, and to considerable frustration on the part of reference staff. Reference librarians ask for a lot: more technical support staff, for new electronic products, for physical renovation projects to support technology, and for travel money to attend continuing education programs on technical topics. They want new computer equipment or upgrades, *instant* equipment repairs, and time to learn about the daily changes brought by digital reference products and services. If there is no lab or hands-on learning classroom, they want a lab or classroom, and if there is one, they want a better-equipped facility, with the newest projection systems, video integration, and the fastest network connectivity. There is usually not enough money to do all this, or at least to do it as quickly and seamlessly as it ought to be done. Again, there are solutions.

Association of Research Libraries annual statistics show a slow trend toward more money being spent on operating costs and less on staff.[8] This is no doubt due to the fact that technology is not usually funded through budget enhancements, but rather from reallocation of existing budgets. Most libraries attempt to protect the collection budgets (although more of that protected budget is spent on digitally produced purchases and licenses) and the only other budget categories are staff and operating. Therefore, when operating costs rise substantially due to the demands for new technologies, the only place to find the funding is from salary lines. When positions are vacant (even if they are not intentionally held vacant permanently), much of the savings is going toward funding computer equipment, technology-related facility renovation, and other such costs. In some cases, funding that previously supported permanent staff lines is being moved to temporary staffing arrangements or contracts. Is this a negative trend? Not necessarily. In the world of reference or public catalog web development, some reference departments are finding that the best thing to do is to contract with a website development company. Others are hiring part time student webmasters to maintain links on preestablished library web sites. Others are investing in software that promises to do that work automatically, cruising for URLs in 856 fields and trying them out. Dollars that collect in lapsing salary funds during vacancies are perfect to fund these sorts of solutions. Librarians can easily understand these budget management techniques and may even help find ways to generate additional flexible funds that had been previously locked into salaries.

Another type of solution is found through partnerships. In a university, specific needs felt by academic departments or divisions may be jointly funded, either through internal funds or through sponsored research or other outside grants. In a consortium, a single technician can be on call for multiple libraries or can be scheduled to complete projects requested by member libraries on a priority basis. Or, an outside contract for hardware support can be funded jointly by more than one unit, such as the library and the computer center.

Finally, while it requires considerable effort up front, fund raising through grants and gifts is a real possibility for technology-based projects. Even long-term projects can be funded through grants, since endowment revenues can be used on an ongoing basis for staffing, funding of site licenses, and other annual costs. Federal funds are available for innovative uses of information technology, demonstration and model projects, and for advancement of networked resources, through agencies and funding programs. Examples are: LSTA (administered by state libraries in most cases, so check your state library's website), NEH <http://www.neh.fed.us>, NEA <http://arts.endow.gov/Homepage/Homepage.html>, TIAAP <http://www.ntia.doc.gov>, NSF <http://www.nsf.gov>, and IMLS <http://www.imls.fed.us>. Foundation grants for library technology projects are also available, and many leads are found guides to library fund raising, such as the recent work edited by Elizabeth Rich.[9] In higher education, most universities and colleges engage in active institutional advancement or development work, and in many cases, libraries (including larger public libraries) now have their own development directors. In schools with centralized development offices, a reference librarian with a good idea may be able to get help from a professional grant writer. Even if the reference department must be directly involved in writing up a proposal, it may be far easier than you think to prepare a gift or grant request–some foundations do not want a proposal longer than three or four pages. However, outside funding for projects may bring a long-term problem. It is very common for grants to fund the purchase of equipment for a lab or bibliographic instruction space on a one-time basis. Three years later, the library will have a problem with microcomputers without enough space for current software, or with slow telecommunication connections. While most libraries go ahead with one-time funds for projects and equipment whenever they can, fewer solve the problem of ongoing maintenance, upgrade, and replacement through endowments and gifts. It is more common for libraries to find ways to re-allocate existing resources for those ongoing operating costs of delivering reference services.

Planning for Technical Support and Reference Staffing

Among the most troublesome issues for reference staffs are technical support and staffing levels. The systems office of the library can never respond quickly enough, can't be there late at night, and may be staffed with amateur troubleshooting students working on a part time basis with limited training. Even taking the time to report all the technical problems can be challenging when the reference librarian is facing a queue of patrons waiting for help at the desk. Yet, communication with the library systems or technical support office is really critical. The library must have a reliable trouble reporting system. The systems staff should have a way to assess the urgency of the problem, or to rate the criticality of the fix. In a small library, technical support may be coming from a volunteer who already has a full time position. In a middle sized library, a single full or part time position may be attempting to support the local area network and all equipment hooked up to it. In a larger library, a combination of full and part time or student staff may be undertaking a full range of program development, planning, troubleshooting an integrated library system, and system upgrade responsibilities. In some cases, the library is fully supported by a central computer center staff. It is likely that no matter which of these scenarios fits your library, the reference department feels the level of technical support is not adequate. After all, the information professional at the reference desk is usually focussed on the information content that meets the needs of library users, rather than the management of the information systems or the telecommunication infrastructure. Of course, this professional orientation is changing as schools of library and information science re-structure their curricula to include more material on computer systems, software and telecommunications. More librarians than ever are fully capable of solving even difficult technical problems, writing programs, doing sophisticated web sites, and creating new ways to use new tools in support of information services. More librarians enjoy these challenges as much as the challenge of finding the best answer to a reference question or designing a successful and popular instructional seminar. Even given this change in technical ability, which increases the likelihood that the reference librarian and the technically skilled librarian are one and the same, there is an undeniable need for systems support staff for reference and bibliographic programs. Sometimes, the reference department may be large enough to warrant dedicated technical staff to support user workstations, CD networks, public catalog interfaces, and public printing systems. Regardless of the circumstances, funding for more technical staff will be needed as new programs are designed and implemented. Workloads everywhere in the library will need to be examined to decide how positions can be redeployed to meet these needs.

Further, each reference department has to consider finding its own solutions to staffing needs, facing the question of whether or not service is improved with paraprofessionals, library science students, or professionals such as catalogers. Each department must decide whether there should be a separate information or technical troubleshooting desk or whether to invest in a training program for student assistants who will "rove" among user workstations offering help with resources linked to the library web-site. Each reference department has to work out an agreement about the sort of queries that can be referred to the computer center help desk. It is especially important to discuss strategies for staffing *new* services (creation of electronic reserves, e-mail reference, web links to online catalog use tips), or outreach services for new user populations (corporate information management training programs, digital document delivery, off-site instructional seminars, programs for new academic departments launched to meet changing needs). Sometimes, it is necessary for priorities to be set, and a reference department may decide to phase out previously supported programs (such as a library research handbook's 4th edition) or services (such as the introductory bibliographic instruction seminar for brand new first year students, or library orientation tours on audiotape). Canceling a service or program can generate hundreds of hours for new program development and implementation. Choices like this are hard, especially when information professionals have invested years of effort into long-supported but no longer state of the art programs. But choices are part of planning for change.

Specific Program Planning

As mentioned above, each new program or project requires in-depth planning. Grant writing, budget allocation or re-allocation, staffing, equipment purchases, ongoing maintenance, training, continuing education, and program assessment are all key stages in planning. Some stages are more important than others for technology assisted reference services.

Services for nontraditional students such as adult learners, off-campus students, students engaged in study abroad, and corporate training programs are addressing needs of new higher education markets. As such, libraries and campus administrators should realize that new funding should be available. An important argument for the library is that the university is receiving new tuition dollars from new student markets, so the library should share in that revenue flow, with enhanced funding shared with the academic units generating the programs of learning. All universities do not model budget development on such a decentralized revenue distribution concept. But even in centralized budget distribution models, an understanding of the costs of delivering new services to new student markets can lead to resource sharing among key stakeholders and academic units. Fortunately, libraries are usually well positioned to support basic services for nontraditional students. The online catalog is already accessible from remote computers. Most or all of the collections are reflected in the online catalog. A suite of journal article finding tools often accompanied by commercial document delivery services (Uncover, UMI, etc.) are linked to the library's catalog. Full text resources are available and may be licensed by the library from major vendors such as IAC, OCLC, etc. Interlibrary loan departments already exist, and to some extent can absorb additional workloads because of improved efficiencies offered through such options as the OCLC Interlibrary loan Fee Management program (IFM) identifying added costs, and values; and matching them with new student tuition markets is a good strategy.

Technology-assisted communication, which includes email reference and web-based teaching systems, may be labor-intensive to implement. Pilot projects will help answer important questions such as whether the users of an email reference service are the same individuals who used to visit the desk and are emailing instead, or if they are rather individuals who did not previously use the reference service at all. In short, it is useful to find out how much additional workload is really being created, and how much workload is only being transferred from one service to another. A pilot project can also help establish the most appropriate sort of staffing. If the well-known anonymous question board used at UCLA, University of Illinois, and other undergraduate libraries for years can be staffed with library science students supervised by reference librarians, then can email reference be handled in the same way? Each library may find different results of such a pilot study. A pilot project creating a web version of a standard paper handout can help establish the cost of doing a full program of online help guides. Pilot projects should include some element of feedback or assessment. A focus group giving feedback on a bibliographic instructional PowerPoint presentation can compare the effectiveness of the in-person presentation, and the same presentation available on the library's web site. This could well decide whether or not the reference librarians all make an effort to transform existing teaching materials in multiple formats into multimedia presentations over the campus network. If a decision is made to move ahead with this transformation of instructional material, the reference department should find out the most cost-effective way to achieve results. Can the work be done by a commercial firm, by staff in the computer center who are paid for the project, by a volunteer librarian taking a semester of professional leave, or by the library systems office staff on assignment? Once the work is done, how will it be maintained and updated? Planning, testing, and feedback phases are all critical to effective budget planning and overall implementation success. Similar planning phases must be undertaken for development of new online help systems integrated into online catalogs or gateways to external resources such as journal indexes and full text files.

The Need for Continuing Education

Continuing education for information professionals and reference support staff is a vital necessity. It takes many forms, of course. Travel to national conferences to hear discussion programs and expert speakers is really quite important in order to stay connected to current issues. Participation in regional and local training seminars can enhance the quality of user services. Team building exercises, trust building activities, and peer coaching programs all have their place in a contemporary library organization. But perhaps just as important is individual, personal learning time. Each librarian wants and needs time to read the current issues of important journals in order to absorb the experiences of other libraries, be able to apply published research findings, and put local policy into perspective. Each librarian wants some time to surf the web, identifying and assessing the hundreds of new and valuable resources popping up weekly. Each librarian needs time to "play" with new online resources, new databases, new search engines, and new releases of older products. Listserv reading time can be hard to find, and these media for topical communication can become burdensome, but can often lead to very useful applications of good ideas. Creativity needs to be fed and supported through this sort of time. Unfortunately, this kind of time is rare and needs to be fitted into not only the librarian's workweek but also his or her life in general. But both programmatic and personal learning is key to maintaining a confident, capable, and professionally connected reference department. Both are critical to good morale. Both should be scheduled and, whenever possible, funded through continuing education funds, professional travel funds, and funds for release time and substitute staffing.

In conclusion, there are many components to planning for effective uses of technology in delivering reference and instructional services in libraries. Planning takes time and effort, collaboration and creativity. With appropriate emphasis on planning, the promise of improvements in quality of services through information technologies can and should become a reality.

REFERENCES

1. Twigg, Carol A. and Diana G. Oblinger, *The Virtual University: A Report from a Joint Educom/IBM Roundtable*, Washington D.C., November 5-6, 1996, <http://www.educom.edu/nlii/VU.html>.

2. Diaz, Karen R., "User Success in a Networked Environment," *RQ*, v. 36, no. 3, Spring, 1997, pp. 393-407.

3. Jewell, Tim, and Martha Kyrillidou, "Research Library Investments in Electronic Resources," a project report presented at the Spring, 1997 Coalition on Networked Information meeting, April 1-2, Washington DC.

4. Simmons, Elizabeth A., and Randall M. MacDonald. "Reference Services and Collection Development: Faculty Outreach through the Campus Network." *The Reference Librarian*, no. 58, 1997, pp. 101-106.

5. *Innovations in Education and Training International*, Nov. 1997, v. 34, no. 4.

6. Mendelsohn, Jennifer. "Perspectives on Quality of Reference Service in an Academic Library: A Qualitative Study." *RQ*, Summer 1997, v. 36, no. 4 pp. 544-557.

7. Orr, Debby, Margaret Appleton, and Trish Andrews, "Teaching Information Literacy Skills to Remote Students Through an Interactive Workshop." *Research Strategies*, v. 14, no. 4, 1996, pp. 224-233.

8. Dillon, Martin, "Measuring the Impact of Technology on Libraries; A Discussion Paper," Dublin, OH: OCLC, 1993.

9. Rich, Elizabeth H., ed. *National Guide to Funding for Libraries and Information Services*. New York: Foundation Center, 1997.

Reference Services and Media
in Academic Libraries

Thura R. Mack

SUMMARY. This paper examines the impact of new and developing media on academic libraries, specifically discussing technology which enables video and movie clips to be transferred over intranets and the Internet. This Web technology could have implications for other electronic media and databases, for offering extended services, including training and orientation for new staff and students; and for online library instruction modules. More generally, the article will discuss some issues, ramifications, protocols, and legal implications involved when libraries introduce and implement new multimedia services and other web-based resources. *[Article copies available for a fee from The Haworth Document Delivery Service: 1-800-342-9678. E-mail address: getinfo@haworthpressinc. com]*

KEYWORDS. Multimedia technology, reference services, information technology, electronic media

INTRODUCTION

Over the last ten years, academic libraries have invested in more and more multimedia products, services, and information delivery systems. Making information resources increasingly virtual and wireless, both in libraries and from remote locations, is a driving force that puts equipment, media, and software in a race to provide the "right"

Thura R. Mack is Associate Professor and Reference Librarian, University of Tennessee, John C. Hodges Library, Knoxville, TN 37996-1000.

[Haworth co-indexing entry note]: "Reference Services and Media in Academic Libraries." Mack, Thura R. Co-published simultaneously in *The Reference Librarian* (The Haworth Information Press, an imprint of The Haworth Press, Inc.) No. 65, 1999, pp. 29-38; and: *Reference Services and Media* (ed: Martha Merrill) The Haworth Information Press, an imprint of The Haworth Press, Inc., 1999, pp. 29-38. Single or multiple copies of this article are available for a fee from The Haworth Document Delivery Service [1-800-342-9678, 9:00 a.m. - 5:00 p.m. (EST). E-mail address: getinfo@haworthpressinc.com].

29

combination of elements. The fluidity of information sources causes a frenzy in computer enterprises as each company struggles to gain a leg up on its competition. Nonstop enhancements of software create higher and higher expectations from users and consumers. Librarians, as key stakeholders in this arena, are transforming themselves from providers of traditional materials and services to experts in digital information formats. More specifically, academic libraries are now offering high-tech devices for video and audio streaming that are heavily marketed towards both educational and corporate outlets. This technology can be integrated with Internet and intranet applications, thus revolutionizing library media collections. However, librarians should proceed cautiously as they adopt or implement new technology in their respective libraries or institutions. It is not always imperative to acquire the latest technological developments immediately upon their release. There must be long-range planning and evaluation to gauge the specific needs of library users and the services, materials, and technology required to meet these needs.

IMPACT ON ACADEMIC INSTITUTIONS

Overall institutional support of electronic media or multimedia is just one consideration. Much larger considerations are the financial, political, administrative, and governance issues. Due to unrelenting budget shortfalls, many institutions are having to make tough choices about what to give up and what to keep while simultaneously maintaining adequate levels of service and trying to stay current with technology.

According to Brian Lang ("The Electronic Library," *Libri*, v. 44 no. 3, September 1994, p. 268), "the most serious impediments in these deliberations are not technological. They are commercial, legal, cultural and professional, and include the key issues of academic integrity." As Lang continues to describe these dilemmas, it becomes clear that the major barriers here are intellectual policy rather than technological. When an institution moves forward in the technological discussion, an implicit statement of support is made. A new school of thought comes into play and there is a shift in the normal agenda. For example, the library's role in the academy is no longer as warehouse of sorts; rather, it has become a center of excellence in information management, access, and dissemination, making full use of current multimedia and information technology. These new information delivery modes help the institution facilitate services such as distance learning, online databases, and Web-mounted library collections since the user does not always have to be physically present in the library to retrieve, manipulate, and make use of information resources.

IMPACT ON LIBRARIANS

The good news is, more and more, librarians are instructing users on how to do research with new technologies, thus teaching both content and technology basics. Students and library users will always have varying levels of technical knowledge and skills. Librarians must be able to address these skill levels quickly without creating more anxiety for the users. Audio and video streaming will make it possible for librarians to create more sophisticated tutorial modules and also offers real time audio/video presentation of information (via the Internet, CD-ROM, etc.), which can enhance the appeal and effectiveness to users with varying learning styles.

As librarians assume new roles resulting from technological developments, they must also realistically address concomitant problems, issues, and concerns. Drawbacks include permanence and persistence of some information–will it always be available? Other concerns include data shifting and problems with information integrity which invites the following questions: Are libraries responsible for all information? What kind of technical support is required? Can the library support all of the students' technical needs? Do libraries have all the technologies to support new information demands? Do libraries want to provide all the support for these new technologies? As solutions are being sought for these dilemmas, should libraries continue to do everything for everyone? Obviously systems that expand and improve services must be thoroughly evaluated. Performance measures should clearly take into consideration all stakeholders. Libraries cannot provide support for all new technologies. Technology's multifaceted nature does not allow one establishment to manage all services of information technology. The mindset of librarians shows that with each new development of information systems, we think this will solve all problems; however, new technologies come with unique demands and caveats. A good example of this is the following discussion of multimedia.

ELECTRONIC MEDIA OR MULTIMEDIA INFORMATION DELIVERY FORMATS/SYSTEMS

Since this technology is in a developmental stage, serious consideration must be given to the key issues of protocols, storage, and standards. Costly mistakes could result if service and equipment choices are made without proper research on storage, compatibility with existing technology, and other capabilities. This technology must be locally and nationally compatible, according to existing standards, to be properly integrated with text-based library services.

Literature reviews highlight libraries moving to more sophisticated media and levels of service. Video streaming is used to mount video and movie clips for network delivery, greatly enhancing media services for remote users and distance learners in homes, offices, dorms, and classrooms. Streaming is defined by *WebReference PC Webopaedia* (http://howto.yahoo.com/chapters/6/4.html) as "A technique for transferring data such that it can be processed as a steady and continuous stream," and by Yahoo as "A streamed file which you can start playing before it's finished downloading." Yahoo! also says, "Think of it this way: Instead of sending you an audio or video clip as a single file, it's sent as a series of individual sounds or pictures–a stream of them, if you will."

Companies are designing multimedia delivery systems so that they are compatible with existing technology. The architecture of video streaming is designed to be delivered across platforms, using standard web browsers, HTML, and plug-ins. Streaming video for computers relies on MPEG-1, and for broader bandwidth MPEG-2, to allow delivery and storage of video and audio; additional features are integrated content and storage management options. Intelligent content placement creates indexing so that familiar search strategies such as keyword, subject, and title can be used. This offers scalability, meaning room for growth and massive applications; reliability with built-in programming to minimize system crashes or shutdowns; and system flexibility in price as well as design. Specifications further offer support of Windows 95 (optivision), Windows NT (optibase) and Macintosh (wired).

Since video streaming is an emerging technology, much of the detailed discussions are only available via the web and weekly publications such as *EMedia, PC World, Video, MacWorld,* and *LAN Times.*

As competing streaming technologies surface, it is critical to look closely at the seven layers of the ISO standard (see definitions below). If common standards for communicating systems are not carefully addressed between vendors and libraries, there could be gross incompatibilities between users and providers and between new and existing systems.

1. *physical–* The network and associated hardware; the physical connection and physical hardware/software that drive the process.
2. *datalink–* Types of physical connections both physical connections and standardized protocols exchange of data
3. *network–* A set of interconnected computers whose file systems are linked together; a general term describing a number of connected computers functioning as a single computer.
4. *transports–* Establishes and dissolves connections between hosts
5. *session–* A connection of two nodes on a network, an established communication between two nodes.
6. *presentation–*The part of the whole communication/networking process that tries to translate needs of the different types of devices; in order to get the data ready for output or application.
7. *application–* The part of the networking process that is handled by the actual user's programs.

(Adapted from Mark Norris, *Understanding Networking Technology: Concepts, Terms and Trends*)

Video streaming is most widely used as a commercial business application on closed intranets. Educational institutions are beginning to look at how to use these technologies in order to deliver multi-media more effectively over campus networks. According to Tamara Miller, Head, Planning, The University of Tennessee Libraries, the challenge for librarians is to discover how this technology can improve and extend library services. Reference service, bibliographic instruction, and information service might all be candidates for delivery via networked multimedia. Potentially, a library could reach more people at the exact point of need if users could initiate a specific multimedia based library service when they need it. Interactive video and desktop teleconferencing could allow libraries to extend valuable reference services beyond the reference room. The sensible use of the technology must be driven by the mission of the library and the needs of users. Miller is spearheading a pilot project at the University of Tennessee using *Black Athena* and *Search for Solutions* as demo videos. These videos were digitized and loaded onto a video server for student viewing at PCs, in classrooms or in the university main library. Also, discussions and planning are underway for designing web-based tutorials at the University of Tennessee.

According to Rick Provine, Director of Media and Electronic Center Services at the University of Virginia, audio and video streaming is being tested, but with some elements in production. First, the library was able to introduce and help implement video streaming technology for the Curry School of Education to provide an online continuing education program, called CaseNet, to support case-based teaching. Audio streaming is used to deliver online sound effects from a library database. Users can preview the sound before making time-consuming downloading decisions. The university is currently exploring delivery of music digitizing William Faulkner's lectures from his tenure as Writer in Residence and making them available on audio CD, and soon via the web. Many of these online collections are available only for local access due to intellectual property rights. Mr. Provine thinks the ability to deliver audio and video to desktops via streaming technology will enhance development of course materials by integrating varying types of data.

At a recent software product demonstration at The University of Tennessee, Silicon Graphics displayed and discussed their multimedia product, Media Base. This software is still in the testing phase but is designed to support audio and video streaming. According to the company representatives, it will eventually be used on a personal computer via CD-ROM or the web. They indicated that bandwidth capability/compatibility is the major problem area right now.

Though bandwidth capability/compatibility can be problematic, there are ways around this. Real time streaming protocol (RTSP) standardizes a way of compressing header information on streaming video packets traveling between modem-bank terminal adapters and the Internet routers, which reduces bandwidth. Utilizing RTSP provides advantages of bi-direction, enabling full stream control, overhead data delivery, security, intellectual property rights protection, and scalability and design is based on field-proven techniques. Also, Silicon Graphics' video server will let IT (information technology) managers which have RTSP-aware routers reserve specific amounts of bandwidth for RTSP traffic. Another aid to bandwidth problems is the MBONE, a virtual network. It is layered on top of portions of the physical Internet to support routing of IP multicast packets since that function has not yet been integrated into many production routers.

The television industry has been using audio and video streaming since the early 1990s. In Jan Ozer's article, "Streaming Video: The Time is Now," in *EMedia* he describes several products that are available now for business and educational application. He mentions Real-Video by Progressive Network as having the capacity to support video streaming on the internet or intranet. Ozer compares technologies of VDOLive, ClearVideo, RealVideo, VXtreme's Web Theater, and VivoActive, looking at compatibilities and effectiveness in both traditional and non-traditional environments. The good news is these video software products on web sites start at moderate prices.

It comes as no surprise that library services are greatly enhanced by emerging technologies. With selective tweaking, these resources can become discipline-, user-, or institution-specific, as well as general. As librarians juggle numerous instructional needs (i.e., subject based, general orientation, etc.), we cannot do everything all the time, but mechanisms such as electronic media and multimedia can enable us to cope. Implementing new technologies allows us to offer an explicit new level of service. A significant feature of web-based services is that libraries can at last make services available to users 24 hours a day, seven days a week. Critical impediments to instruction exist currently because general library orientation classes are offered at busy times for many students (who are in class, at work, or in a lab) during regular eight-to-five time slots. Making information and service more available allows students to easily tap into resources at the point of need.

COPYRIGHT

According to Arlene Bielefield and Lawrence Cheeseman, authors of *Libraries & Copyright Law* published by Neal-Schuman Publishers in 1993, copyright is "the group of fundamental rights given to authors of creative works for a limited period of time." Laura Gasaway and Sarah Wiant describe copyright by what it does, i.e., "A copyright grants to its owner the right to control an intellectual or artistic creation, to prohibit other persons from using that work in specific ways without permission and to profit from the sale and performance of the work." More, specifically they say that "if the programs are authored and created via computer, then the copyright, in the end, would probably belong to the employer."

As new technologies arise, copyright laws expand to include them. Some commonly used terms that index information on copyright and current technology are: Internet–Legal use, Internet–Business use, Copyright–Computer-stored information, Communications Decency Act, Telecommunications–Legal aspects, and Telecommunications Act of 1996. Copyright laws must address the electronic environment and intellectual property, trademarks, privacy, taxation, equity of access, display, publication, adaptation and reproduction.

PARTNERSHIPS

Today's technological changes necessitate the creation of partnerships and alliances. Privatizing new technical services and supporting roles is a natural business solution for making available new technology and multimedia delivery requires various applications of hardware and software systems. To increase productivity businesses are forming partnerships across industry lines, from the development stage to monitoring of a new product's performance. Libraries are looking at partnerships with vendors in order to share the costs of technology and materials, increase technical service support, and capitalize on other available resources outlined in partnership agreements. Ultimately, well-planned partnerships can result in new knowledge and joint product development. According to Gasaway and Wiant, "License agreements typically govern what the owner of a copy of software may do with that program." Within that framework they continue "issues such as warranties, software delivery and upgrades, payment terms," etc. More specifically, site and network licenses determine how many users may access a software or database package simultaneously, and "a site license might restrict the number of computers on which the software may be used at one or more geographic locations." Network licenses cover the use of software or database packages mounted on a server and accessed by users in either campus-wide networks or local area networks (LANs) such as individual labs, buildings, departments, or offices. Video streaming technology will certainly require these types of licensing agreements.

Licensing is inevitably becoming a larger and larger part of intellectual property and legal issues relating to information technology. Librarians are challenged to fit these legal and licensing negotiations into the acquisitions and collection development processes, and they must become more and more proficient in doing so. According to Robert Wedgeworth, former Executive Director of ALA and now University Librarian and Professor of Library Administration, "Librarians must be able to do their own negotiations with many legal licensing deals. Many of these legal deals are not being made in the best interests of consumers (i.e., libraries), therefore, librarians and libraries must assert their own power."

CONCLUSION

Emerging multimedia technology shows great promise for instructional and research capabilities of libraries and academia in general. We must seriously and thoughtfully investigate storage and archiving of information and data available via multimedia formats. While we want to provide as much state-of-the-art technology, services, and information access as possible, we must be careful to consider all of the pros and cons related to implementation of new products. With funding resources becoming more limited, the cost benefit ratio of new technology must be carefully considered. It is crucial that both librarians and other stakeholders be major decision makers for purchase of new information systems and products. We must not let vendors and publishers push new technology upon us without considering all possible ramifications for users, librarians, faculty and staff. Again, long-range planning is the best way to implement new technology and related services to avoid bad decisions and costly mistakes.

The development of policies for licensing and managing electronic information and resources is also a vital component of implementing emerging multimedia technology in libraries. The Association of Research Libraries has pulled together a number of academic and special librarians, library administrators, and library organizations to develop guidelines and principles for drafting and implementing such policies.

ARL has produced two very useful flyers–*Checklist for Drafting Electronic Information Policies* (prepared by Gerald R. Lowell, University of California-San Diego; Paula T. Kaufman, University of Tennessee-Knoxville; and the ARL Information Policies Committee) and *Principles for Licensing Electronic Resources* (prepared by the ARL Working Group formed of a member from the six international associations ARL has charged to look at licensing and related issues). These two publications provide information and guidance to libraries, outlining the various issues (legal and otherwise), values, principles, processes, resources, agreements, etc., to consider as they develop policies and guidelines governing multi-media and other electronic resources. The flyers also include websites of sample policies and other resources relating to electronic resources policies and licensing. The information in the *Principles* flyer can be found at www.arl.org/scomm/licensing/principles.html and the *Checklist* can be obtained from ARL (21 Dupont Circle, NW, Washington, DC 20036).

REFERENCES

1. American Association of Law Libraries et al. (July 15, 1997). *Principles for Licensing Electronic Resources* (Final Draft).

2. Association of Research Libraries et al. (1998). *Checklist For Drafting Electronic Information Policies* (Final Draft).

3. Barrier, Michael (1997), Don't get caught in the net's web. *Nation's Business*, p. 22-24.

4. Bielefield, Arlene and Lawrence Cheesemanm (1993). *Libraries & Copyright Law*. New York: Neal-Schuman Publishers, Inc.

5. Gasaway, Laura N. and Sarah K. Wiant (1994). *Libraries and copyright: A guide to copyright law in the 1990s*. Washington, D.C.: Special Libraries Association.

6. Lang, Brian (1994), The electronic library: Implications for librarians, academics and publishers. *Libri*, 44, p. 256-71.

7. Ozar, Jan (1997), Streaming video: The time is now. *EMedia Professional, 10*, p. 44-45.

8. Web Community (12/19/98). *Yahoo* [http://howto.yahoo.com/chapters/6/4. html].

"Going Where the Questions Are": Using Media to Maintain Personalized Contact in Reference Service in Medium-Sized Academic Libraries

Sarah Brick Archer
Melissa Cast

SUMMARY. Different approaches to reference service have been added over the years, but the basic premise of the service has not changed–the desire to assist and educate users in locating information. As new technologies are added, such as desktop conferencing and web access, it is important that the personalized contact which is the heart of reference service be preserved. The human touch in the reference process is very important to the success of the reference transaction. Media can be useful in assisting reference librarians in "Going Where the Questions Are" while still maintaining the personal element in creating real-time reference transactions in a technological environment. *[Article copies available for a fee from The Haworth Document Delivery Service: 1-800-342-9678. E-mail address: getinfo@haworthpressinc.com]*

Sarah Brick Archer is Reference Co-Coordinator and Arts and Letters Resource Coordinator, and Melissa Cast is Refereence Librarian and Education Resource Coordinator, both at the John Vaughan Library, Northeastern State University, 711 North Grand, Tahlequah, OK 74464-2398 (E-mail: archersa@cherokee.nsuok.edu or castma@cherokee.nsuok.edu).

[Haworth co-indexing entry note]: "'Going Where the Questions Are': Using Media to Maintain Personalized Contact in Reference Service in Medium-Sized Academic Libraries." Archer, Sarah Brick, and Melissa Cast. Co-published simultaneously in *The Reference Librarian* (The Haworth Information Press, an imprint of The Haworth Press, Inc.) No. 65, 1999, pp. 39-50; and: *Reference Services and Media* (ed: Martha Merrill) The Haworth Information Press, an imprint of The Haworth Press, Inc., 1999, pp. 39-50. Single or multiple copies of this article are available for a fee from The Haworth Document Delivery Service [1-800-342-9678, 9:00 a.m. - 5:00 p.m. (EST). E-mail address: getinfo@haworthpressinc.com].

KEYWORDS. Reference service, video conferencing, reference interview, electronic resources

INTRODUCTION

Reference librarians need to consider ways to be more accessible to all users and maintain personalized contact. Just as there are different learners, library clients need different approaches to reference service. The roving librarian serves the on-site user, while kiosks, video conferencing, and web access address the needs of remote users. In Fall of 1997, the Reference Department of Northeastern State University coined the slogan, "Going Where the Questions Are" to serve as a banner to improve service to all reference department library users. Many of the techniques utilize different types of media and can be effective in medium-sized academic libraries which, because of their size, are more able to adopt these approaches.

BACKGROUND

In early librarianship, assistance wasn't even provided to library patrons. "The father of the American reference process, Samuel Green, instituted the first formal reference service at the Worcester Public Library in Massachusetts in 1876."[1] In the 1800s, librarians saw the need to help patrons locate and interpret library finding tools. The reference librarian was born.

Libraries developed centralized reference desks where reference librarians waited for questions to come to them. Some academic libraries instituted departmental libraries.

A few academic libraries, such as Brandeis University, have removed the librarians from the reference desk and librarians are mainly available for consultations. This provides in-depth, uninterrupted assistance for the user.[2] This seems to be effective for graduate libraries, but may not be as effective in serving students in medium-sized academic libraries.

Whether the Reference Department has changed or the customers' needs have changed, the primary emphasis of reference to guide and teach people to use resources hasn't changed. Different clients have different needs from the Reference Department, and additional modes of service have been added over the years, such as phone and e-mail reference. None of these have replaced traditional face-to-face interaction between reference librarian and library patron. Some students who live on campus might prefer a face-to-face interaction with a librarian. Other students might communicate more effectively in writing and prefer contacting the Reference Department via computer. There are, however, several approaches that can improve all types of reference service. No matter where the patron is, we need to "Go Where the Questions Are," and answer the questions effectively and professionally. Reference librarians must emphasize our strengths which are our combination of people and technology skills. The manner in which we answer the question can be as important as providing factual information.

Telephone reference has been done for years and is a great way to use media in reference. The reference interview can be highly effective and the question can be answered in real time. There are also new phones available that free the librarian's hands to locate reference books or type on keyboards. The benefits of the librarian's good people skills shine in this environment.

"Going Where the Questions Are" can be accomplished by going directly to faculty offices to answer questions. If a faculty member is having difficulty using electronic reference tools from her office, go to the professor's office and provide a little one-on-one tutoring. One librarian at Northeastern State University took an ERIC thesaurus to the faculty member's office and talked the professor through the research process.

Another way to reach students would be to place signs in computer labs listing the reference desk phone number and offering reference assistance. The same information could be listed on menu screens embedded in computer programs, CD-ROM LANs, or the World Wide Web. With this approach, the librarian is accessible from other locations on campus without ever leaving the library.

THE ROVING LIBRARIAN

Service to on-site library patrons is still provided in medium-sized academic libraries by reference librarians sitting at a reference desk waiting for questions to come to them. This puts the burden on the student to come to the reference desk. As the student approaches the reference desk, the librarian often appears to be too busy typing on a keyboard or reading to be considered approachable by the patron.

One way to improve this traditional approach to reference assistance is to implement the concept of "Going Where the Questions Are" by using roving librarians. With this approach, reference librarians are still available at the reference desk, but other assistants roam the floor looking for patrons who need assistance. This approach can be helpful to the students because they don't have to stop what they were doing and leave their workstations to get assistance. They receive immediate help and don't have to "interrupt" busy librarians. Boston College Library, who used staff from other areas of the library as rovers, found that the reference librarians benefitted by the extra assistance and that it saved them time in running from the reference desk to the workstations.[3]

Boston College found that three-fourths of the rover interactions lasted less than five minutes. This personalized approach to "Going Where the Questions Are" was a benefit to both students and librarians. In a survey done by Boston College, "overall 90% of the users said they found the information they needed. This high success rate has led to greater user satisfaction and reduced demands on the staff."[4]

The roving librarian model was also tried at Utica College in New York. One important point raised in their study is that the roving librarian reaches patrons who would not use the traditional reference service provided at the reference desk. "One especially surprising result is the almost complete lack of overlap between roving and passive reference encounters."[5] Roving librarianship expands reference service by reaching clients with a need for proactive librarianship.

Many students are shy or do not want to admit that they need help. Forcing them to approach a reference desk only increases the students' anxiety level. As Utica College found, "Unfortunately, the official reference desk survey also shows that reference service reaches only a tiny fraction of library users."[6]

The roving librarian appeared to be more in touch with the problems encountered by the students trying to use electronic resources. One of the most common problems was students using inappropriate databases. "Roving reference offers a greater chance for librarians to teach users the techniques that make improved searching possible."[7] The types of questions answered by Utica College's roving librarian were different than the ones answered by the reference desk librarians. While the roving librarians helped select the most relevant database, the reference desk librarians were locating specific items.[8]

The Utica College study indicated that roving reference service reaches more students. The level of questions handled by the roving librarian appeared to be more sophisticated than the questions asked at the reference desk.

In our effort to improve reference service by using a personalized approach to "Go Where the Questions Are," the roving librarian model seems to be a real plus. By standing, rather than sitting, by approaching the students first, rather than forcing them to approach us, we increase the students' access to our professional reference assistance. Going to the students, making the initial contact is one effective way to improve reference service in a medium-sized academic library.

DESKTOP CONFERENCING/REAL-TIME REFERENCE

Another way to "Go Where the Questions Are" and maintain the human element of reference service involves desktop conferencing. The Center for Business Information at Emory University in Atlanta experimented with the AT&T Vistium Desktop Video system to assist students at remote sites. This system is similar to distance education systems and requires a camera, telephone box, microphone, codex, application-sharing software, and Windows. "Initially, the system crashed frequently. . . . We discovered that the application sharing software was very sensitive."[9] Lighting has to be considered for the image on camera to be effective.

Patron reactions to the system were interesting. For instance it was determined that ". . . not everyone likes to be on camera."[10] Some patrons even covered the screen. Perhaps such high visibility can be a little too personal for some library users. However, there seems to be potential for desktop video conferencing because it is a way to stay in touch with those patrons physically removed from the library.

The Science Library at the University of California, Irvine experimented with desktop video conferencing to provide real-time reference. Since 1996, they have been using CU-SeeMe software in a

Macintosh environment. One project goal was to integrate the interactive reference service into the reference desk functions including drop-in service, telephone reference, consultation-by-appointment and electronic reference.[11]

Video conferencing is an interesting approach to providing real-time reference because of the audio and video capabilities. Databases can be displayed as well as written text, such as sharing search strategies with the student. "Being able to see the video image of the person on the other end of the connection adds a personal and friendly aspect to the interchange."[12]

At the Northeastern State University library, the Reference Department has been trying to meet the information needs of students at a satellite campus library that does not have a professional librarian on site. With the goal of providing personalized service, the department proposed a pilot project to enable a reference librarian at the main campus to see and manipulate the computer screen, and communicate verbally, with a student at the satellite campus.

"PC Anywhere" (version 8, 32 bit for Windows 95) was chosen as the software to manipulate the computer screen. "Internet Phone" and the Netscape communication software have been suggested for the auditory component of the project. A beta test site is proposed to be ready by the fall of 1998. If this is successful, the reference librarian will have used media to "Go Where the Questions Are" and maintain the human element.

The Internet Public Library is providing real-time reference through the web in a Multi-User Object Oriented Environment (MOO).[13] It first began as an experiment in Fall of 1995. Originally, it was accessible through Telnet, but now it is available through the World Wide Web. Several problems were identified with the original experiment. There were patron difficulties in learning commands, confusion with multiple users, concerns over typing, and getting cut off.[14]

In comparing MOO reference with the traditional reference experience, "several librarians commented that on-line reference would not substitute for face to face interviews but that on evenings, or weekends or in remote areas it provided a good alternative."[15] Some suggestions for improving the MOO included simplifying commands and using an IRC chat line.

INTERNET MEDIA

The proliferation of the World Wide Web and the ease of design with html editors provides an additional means for "Going Where the Questions Are." Library hours, staff directories and collection descriptions are found all over the web. Basic information is then readily available for patrons both in and outside of the library. For instance, the Sterling C. Evans Library at Texas A&M University has a virtual tour.[16] Virtual visitors have two options for learning about the library: the Walking Tour or the Point of Interest Tour. With both options, patrons and potential patrons have access to basic information about the library and its services.[17]

Libraries often try to personalize services by using the World Wide Web to make select electronic resources available to their community, as well as create unique new ones. The J. Y. Joyner Library at East Carolina University used a Microsoft-Excel-based database program to develop an in-house periodicals index to many North Carolina state titles not covered by major indexes.[18] Subject headings are based on Library of Congress and Boolean commands are recognized. Accessible from around the world, the index has enabled the library to extend its reach.[19]

With technology abounding and the ease of making information available electronically, it is often easy to lose the human connection. As librarians know, it is not enough to just supply access to information. Distant patrons may often feel lost without assistance readily available from an actual person. As discussed earlier, libraries have traditionally relied on phone service to "Go Where the Questions Are." Additionally, e-mail has developed into a means of reaching those individuals, as well as, a means to increase services. The question for librarians is how to develop effective systems for responding to the electronic information requests, decide who can be served and to what extent we assist them.

Moore identified four models for the management of electronic information requests. In the first model, the questions are answered by the librarian who is responsible for the system. If the numbers of questions grow, additional librarians may assist the first librarian. With the second model, the Head of Reference distributes the questions. In the third model, the questions go to a department e-mail account and the questions are answered on a first-come first-served basis. A bulletin board service (BBS) is used in the fourth model. Questions are forwarded to the BBS and volunteer librarians answer them on a first-come first served basis.[20]

The Internet Public Library has developed a system called QRC to help manage their e-mail reference questions. Designed so it may be easily used by patrons and their volunteer librarians, QRC serves as a mode of communication between patrons and librarians and also as a site for the librarians to coordinate, share and record their work. Categories are designed to hold different types of messages. Forms and e-mail addresses are created to feed the messages to QRC. Messages are called "items," and all subsequent messages pertaining to the item such as responses from the librarians and from the patron are added to the item. The librarian in charge of the item may mark it for inclusion in the archive when the transaction is completed.[21]

As reference e-mail services grow, the community reference librarians serve has the potential to expand greatly. Many medium-sized academic libraries are already struggling with limited staff and their librarians hardly need another responsibility. Some libraries specifically state that they offer limited services to individuals outside of their service community. Even a research library, such as the University of Texas at Austin, indicates on their *Ask a Reference Librarian*, "If you are not affiliated with UT Austin, expect a reply only about unique resources of the General Libraries."[22] The page also informs users that the service is for "asking short, factual questions" and even has a hotlink to a page explaining what a short, factual question is.[23]

Others, like Internet Public Library, place few restrictions on who they will serve. However, they do note on their *Ask a Question at the IPL Reference Center* page that sometimes they may not be able to answer a reference question because too many questions have already been received or because it may require resources unavailable to Internet Public Library. Additionally, Internet Public Library states what level of service the user can expect. Factual questions will receive brief factual answers. Broad questions will receive a list of resources to consult for the topic.[24]

Both the Internet Public Library and the University of Texas at Austin state the level of reference service they provide. Other libraries have separate forms for different services. Creighton University's Health Science Library has a general reference question form[25] and a separate form for literature searches.[26] In each case, the level of reference service is clear. As demand from distant patrons increases, each library should decide what level of reference it is able and willing to provide. Most librarians can remember patrons who expected everything to be just handed to them. Some librarians feel that, "Librarians must work harder to do tasks for online students that resident students would be expected to do for themselves."[27] However, other librarians are concerned about doing research for students. As librarian Dan Reams pondered in the BI-L listserv, "I wonder where student honor codes, requiring students to do all their own work, collide with this notion of the librarian doing the research for students."[28]

Other questions still exist with e-mail reference questions. For instance, conducting an effective reference interview may require several e-mail messages between patron and librarian. New skills may be needed in an electronic environment. Gone are the nonverbal communication clues and the immediacy of an in-person reference interview that aid a librarian in understanding the patron's needs. With an e-mail reference transaction, many librarians assume they understand the question rather than taking the time to clarify the request. Others may rely on a cycle of questions that take time for the patron to answer and then wait for another response.[29] Often the exchange may be frustrating for the librarian and the patron.

During in-person reference interview, most librarians rely on a practiced approach to understanding a patron's questions. This skill and approach is especially important in an e-mail reference interview. Abels notes that the ideal e-mail reference interview should consist of three messages: statement of the problem by the patron, summarization by the librarian and confirmation by the patron. If clarification is needed, the interview can be extended to five messages to include that process. In order to keep the interview efficient, Abels recommends a systematic approach.[30]

There are two approaches to responding systematically. One is to design a structured reference question form to be completed by the patron. The "Computer Search Request Form" at Creighton University, the Health Sciences Library follows this idea. In addition to describing their request, patrons are asked to indicate the type of search wanted and any limitations or restrictions they might have such as language, date ranges and age groups.[31] The Creighton University's

Health Sciences Library's request form states, "The success of the search depends on how succinctly and thoroughly you describe your topic. Please don't just list 'key words' or indicate a search strategy. A succinct description of what you want and why you want it is the most useful information you can provide our staff."[32]

The second approach involves handling an unstructured question. If a patron sends an unstructured question, it is up to the librarian to provide structure. Abels recommends either responding with a standard request form or with questions written in an organized and logical manner, such as a numbered list. In the latter option, patrons may be instructed to respond by referring to the question's number.[33]

Eventually, World Wide Web reference assistance needs to be available in real-time mode where the librarian is alerted to an incoming question, and the patron and librarian can converse without cumbersome commands. The librarian needs to be able to do multi-tasking and show databases while conversing with the student. In the future, perhaps the flexibility of the World Wide Web will be combined with the attributes of desktop conferencing.

CONCLUSION

For years, reference librarians have assumed the role of intermediary between information and patrons. Since information and patrons are no longer just available at the physical library, librarians have needed to adjust their methods of providing service. As any librarian who's been asked a reference question while doing her grocery shopping knows, questions no longer just walk up to the Reference Desk. They are in the stacks, across campus, on the other side of town and maybe outside of the country. To continue to serve patrons with different needs, librarians must walk across the library, access the computer screen from across the campus intranet system, answer e-mail and explore other interactive tools for reaching our patrons in a personalized manner. With changing technologies and new medias, our responsibilities to serve our diverse customers will grow, and as a result, we will have to change to find and utilize new efficient means of meeting those responsibilities.

REFERENCES

1. William Katz, *Introduction to Reference Work*, Volume I (New York: McGraw-Hill, 1978), 5.

2. Douglas Herman, "But Does It Work? Evaluating the Brandeis Reference Model," *Reference Services Review*, Winter 1994, 17-28.

3. Adeane Bregman and Barbara Mento, "Reference Roving at Boston College," *College and Research Libraries News*, November 1992, 635.

4. Ibid.

5. Eileen H. Kramer, "Why Roving Reference: A Case Study in a Small Academic Library," *Reference Services Review*, Fall 1996, 70.

6. Ibid, 71.

7. Ibid, 74.

8. Ibid, 79.

9. Ruth A. Pagell, "The Virtual Reference Librarian: Using Desktop Videoconferencing for Distance Reference, *The Electronic Library*, February 1996, 23.

10. Ibid, 25

11. Susan Lessick, Kathryn Kjaer, Steve Clancy "Interactive Reference Service (IRS) at UC Irvine: Expanding Reference Service Beyond the Reference Desk," Online. 1997 [Available: http://www.ala.org/acrl/paperhtm/a10.html] 4 May 1998.

12. Ibid.

13. "Reference Services in the IPL MOO," Online. 2 March 1998 [Available: http://www.ipl.org/moo] 30 April 1998.

14. Elizabeth Shaw, "Real-Time Reference in a MOO: Promise and Problems," Online. April 1996 [Available: http://www-personal.si.umich.edu/~ejshaw/research2.html] 30 April 1998.

15. Ibid.

16. Pixey Anne Mosley and Daniel Xiao, "Touring the Campus Library from the World Wide Web," *Reference Services Review*, Winter 1996, 7.

17. "Virtual Library Tour," Online. [Available: http://www.tamu.edu/library/reference/virtual/tour00.html] 17 April 1998.

18. Maurice C. York, "Value-Added Reference Service: The North Carolina Periodicals Index," *Computers in Libraries*, May 1997, 30-31.

19. "North Carolina Periodicals Index," Online. January 1998 [Available: http://www.lib.ecu.edu/Periodicals/NCindex/scope.html] 29 April 1998.

20. Amanda Moore, "As I Sit Studying: WWW-Based Reference Services," *Internet Reference Services Quarterly*, 1998, 30-31.

21. Nettie Lagace and Michael McClennen, "QRC: We Call It Quirk," *Computers in Libraries*, February 1998, 26-27.

22. "Ask a Reference Question," Online. 19 March 1997 [Available: http://www.lib.utexas.edu/ask/eref.html] 29 April 1998.

23. Ibid.

24. "Ask a Question at the IPL Reference Center," Online. 19 December 1997 [Available: http://www.ipl.org/ref/QUE/] 4 May 1998.

25. "Reference Service Request Form," Online. [Available: http://tern.creighton.edu/RefForm.html] 1 May 1998.

26. "Computer Search Request Form," Online. [Available: http://tern.creighton.edu/SrchForm.html] 1 May 1998.

27. Ron Chepesiuk, "Internet College: The Virtual Classroom Challenge." *American Libraries*, March 1998, 55.

28. Dan Ream, (1998, April 28). "Re: Off Campus Library Services Conference," [Discussion] BI-L, Online. Available E-Mail: BI-L%bingvmb.bitnet@UGA.edu [April 29, 1998].

29. Eileen G. Abels, "The E-mail Reference Interview," *RQ*, Spring 1996, 348-354.

30. Ibid., 351-354.

31. Ibid., 352.

32. "Computer Search Request Form," Online. [Available: http://tern.creighton.edu/SrchForm.html] 1 May 1998.

33. Abels, 351.

Videoconferencing
and Remote Application Sharing
for Distant Reference Service

Robert B. McGeachin

SUMMARY. Computer technology has progressed to the point where desktop videoconferencing with personal computers and remote application sharing software can be employed in remote reference library service. These technologies can be used to provide personal and effective distant reference and library instruction services to library users, in addition to such traditional methods as mail, telephone, and e-mail service. This article presents scenarios in which videoconferencing and remote applications sharing software can be used in distant reference service. Free software discussed includes CU-SeeMe for videoconferencing and NetMeeting for videoconferencing and remote applications sharing. *[Article copies available for a fee from The Haworth Document Delivery Service: 1-800-342-9678. E-mail address: getinfo@haworthpressinc.com]*

KEYWORDS. Reference service, videoconferencing, remote control software

Traditional methods of interacting with remote reference clients have included mail, telephone calls and more recently e-mail. But all of these methods lack the important element of visual contact that can be crucial for conducting a reference interview that elicits the true

Robert B. McGeachin is Agriculture Reference Librarian, West Campus Library, Texas A&M University, College Station, TX 77843-5001.

[Haworth co-indexing entry note]: "Videoconferencing and Remote Application Sharing for Distant Reference Service." McGeachin, Robert B. Co-published simultaneously in *The Reference Librarian* (The Haworth Information Press, an imprint of The Haworth Press, Inc.) No. 65, 1999, pp. 51-60; and: *Reference Services and Media* (ed: Martha Merrill) The Haworth Information Press, an imprint of The Haworth Press, Inc., 1999, pp. 51-60. Single or multiple copies of this article are available for a fee from The Haworth Document Delivery Service [1-800-342-9678, 9:00 a.m. - 5:00 p.m. (EST). E-mail address: getinfo@haworthpressinc.com].

information needs of the user. Frequently the user does not have a fully defined information need, and the subtle body language cues that a savvy reference librarian can receive in an audio visual interaction can aid in the reference dialog reaching a successful conclusion. The day of the "video phone" that can be used for such audio-video communication has arrived not through commercial telephone service as envisioned by AT&T since the '60s but in the form of the desktop personal computer attached to the Internet with a small digital camera, microphone and appropriate videoconferencing software.

The need for remote reference service has existed for a great while. Those in rural locations at a great distance from any library service have already been making use of remote reference interaction. For example, Land-Grant Universities and the USDA have had experimental stations in rural locations with scientists doing research at them for at least a century. The researchers at these experiment stations need access to scientific literature and information the same as researchers on university campuses or at headquarters locations that have local library service. These remote users have always interacted by mail, then telephone and fax with reference and interlibrary loan librarians. The advent of distance education that is coming to many educational institutions is creating a greatly increased need for remote library circulation, document delivery and remote reference services.

One component of remote library service is the provision of online catalogs, bibliographic databases, and informational databases. For remote users to access these computer products they often require reference assistance to learn how to install, configure and use the appropriate software and frequently need trouble shooting assistance for problems with remote applications. Remote videoconferencing interaction with reference librarians can provide some of this assistance, but another new tool, remote applications sharing or remote control software, can provide very explicit real time instruction, troubleshooting and demonstrating of online resources. Remote access and applications sharing software provides remote control and display of computers and computer applications. For example, the user could be viewing on his computer what the reference librarian is doing with a library database on the library's computer as a form of real time demonstration. If a user is having trouble with a library application, the librarians can view the user's computer to see what is happening and offer appropriate solutions. In some cases actual remote control of the user's computer could be granted to the librarian to fix a problem on the user's computer. A growing number of computer and software manufacturers already offer this kind of remote applications control and remote viewing as a more effective means of troubleshooting user problems by their technical support operations.

A benefit to libraries that can provide remote videoconferencing and remote control software interaction, in addition to having provided better quality service to their users, is the perception by their users that the library is part of the technological forefront. This will be very popular among the technologically comfortable segments of the library's users and a positive public relations gesture. Libraries have been fighting a false perception by the public that they are conservative, stodgy, and technologically behind the times, and this kind of progressive service will help to dispel this notion.

VIDEOCONFERENCING

Until very recently the hardware and software to conduct videoconferencing on desktop PCs was expensive. As digital cameras have become mass consumer items, their prices have dropped to less than $100 for black and white and less than $400 for color. The advent of quality public domain videoconferencing software like CU-SeeMe ™ from Cornell University has driven the market for such software to $100 or less from commercial software publishers. The advent of standards for videoconferencing, H.323 for Internet connections and H.324 for modem to modem links, has created compatible software and hardware from different vendors. Previous to the implementation of these standards only software or modems by the same vendor could usually communicate video with each other. Faster modem speeds of 28,800 bps and higher and better video compression algorithms have allowed the video display quality to improve greatly. Two frames per second refresh rates that are visually jerky have been replaced by ten frames per second or better which have a much smoother appearance. All these factors have converged to make desktop videoconferencing feasible.

Because of the existence of standards, there are a growing number of options available in terms of software and hardware to conduct videoconferencing. Much of the work that has lead to the current feasibility of videoconferencing was done on the Macintosh computer platform. The Macintosh environment has usually been at the forefront of multimedia and graphical computing development in personal computers. But the current dominance of IBM compatible personal computers makes IBM the standard equipment used in most libraries, and specific examples given in this paper will reflect this.

Software is needed to engage in videoconferencing, and one free public domain software videoconferencing application first created by the CU-SeeMe Development Team at Cornell University (1997) is known as CU-SeeMe. It is available to download at URL *http://cu-seeme.cornell.edu*. There are free CU-SeeMe software versions available for the Macintosh, Windows 3.1 (16-bit) and Windows95 and NT (32-bit) operating systems. Minimum IBM PC hardware and software requirements to send and receive audio and video with this software listed at the above site include:

- a 486DX IBM compatible computer
- Windows 3.1 or higher
- a Windows Sockets compliant TCP/IP stack such as Winsock
- a 256 color (8 bit) video driver
- a video capture board that supports Microsoft Video for Windows
- a video camera that plugs into the video capture board
- a Windows sound board compliant to the Windows MultiMedia specification (Sound Blaster or better)
- a microphone
- speakers or headphones
- an Internet connection and IP address

This public domain version of the CU-SeeMe software allows the users to engage in black and white videoconferencing with a two frames per second maximum refresh rate depending on the speed of the Internet connection. But this produces a very jerky video image no where close to the normal 30 frames per second of full motion broadcast and taped video display.

Much better quality is possible with the relatively inexpensive ($100) commercial version of 32-bit CU-SeeMe software from White Pine Software (1998). However, the hardware requirements are such that a costly upgrade from the 486 to Pentium level may be necessary.

The minimum requirements listed by White Pine Software for the latest Version 3.1 for Windows95 or NT 4.0 are as follows:

- Windows95 or NT 4.0
- at least a 100 MHZ Pentium processor
- 16 MB of RAM (24 MB or more recommended)
- 10 MB of free hard disk space for program installation
- a Winsock compliant TCP/IP stack
- an IP address
- either modem (at least a 28.8 Kbps minimum), LAN Ethernet, Cable, or ISDN connection
- PPP for a dial-up connection
- a digital camera (such as a Connectix Quick Cam) or a desktop video camera and video capture board
- a microphone
- a 16-bit minimum sound card and drivers
- speakers or headphones

For reference service by videoconferencing, in addition to equipment in the library, the users must also have video equipment and know how to use it. One early trial attempt at reference service by videoconferencing, at the University of Michigan (Folger, 1997), involved a university library and remote dormitory locations on campus with library satellites. The library established videoconferencing stations at these dorm locations for the students to use with the assistance of library school student workers that staff them. In this manner the users did not have to provide their own equipment, and they had trained help at their end to assist with the sessions. In videoconferencing to library established remote locations, it is important to have trained technical personnel that can troubleshoot any problems that arise for the users. As the population of users becomes more sophisticated, the number with their own video equipment will grow. With knowledge of available applications such as reference service by videoconferencing, the number of users with equipment should increase–"if you build it they will come." Higher education institutions offering distance education may need to require their students to own a sophisticated level of personal computing that includes videoconferencing capabilities to be able to engage in remote classes by desktop videoconferencing. This same equipment could be used for distant library service interaction.

Establishing a videoconferencing reference session requires that both parties have their equipment on and the "calling" users must know the IP address of the library's reference computer to make a connection to it. A library offering reference services by videoconferencing can include its IP address in publicity of the service in addition to its telephone number. In many cases to facilitate connection a phone call to alert reference personnel that a user is attempting to connect is made to ensure that there is someone on the receiving end with his equipment on and ready and in view of the camera. For videoconferencing which is done at the reference desk the use of headphones by the answering librarian can prevent the potential for public disruption that could be caused by speakers. An option to videoconferencing at the reference desk is to establish the service in the offices of reference librarians who are working at their desks but "on call" to take videoconferencing sessions.

The problem of camera shy reference personnel may be encountered. Thorough training and practice in operation of the equipment and software by all reference personnel may partially alleviate this. But it may take longer for some staff to become comfortable with reference service by videoconferencing than others. The same problem of initially camera shy users is overcome with time and successful interactions with the reference personnel on camera. Many cases of initial interactions may just be frivolous "Gee whiz I can do this!" types of sessions with users experimenting with the technology.

In many cases videoconferencing software, such as CU-SeeMe, includes a chat window for written communication. If the audio transmission quality becomes poor, as can occur if Internet traffic becomes too heavy to allow timely delivery of audio and video packets, the chat window can be used to continue the dialog. Difficult concepts or some words in foreign accents may be made clear in writing when they are unintelligible verbally. The chat window can be used to send information like the user's name, address, phone number, IP address and e-mail address for later contact with an answer to a reference question.

REMOTE CONTROL SOFTWARE APPLICATIONS

An even more valuable extension of a shared chat session is the use of remote control or remote application viewing software in reference service. When parties at both ends of a computer session are running the same application sharing software, such as Timbuktu or NetMeeting, they are able to share other computer applications such as bibliographic databases, online catalogs or Internet browser sessions. In such a session communication could already be going on by videoconferencing (or at least telephone if the user is not properly equipped for videoconferencing) and a library software application can be opened and shared by both. The librarian could demonstrate the application which will be on both screens. By the same manner, a user could show the librarian what they are doing for the librarian to troubleshoot a procedural problem the user may be having with the application.

The use of remote control software is already being used by some computer company software support desks to help troubleshoot problems on the caller's computer. With some remote control software it is possible for the person on the remote end of the session to actively control the other computer not just watch what the other end is doing. This type of virtual remote control can be an especially valuable way to allow qualified personnel to actively fix the problem on the other end. Highly trained reference librarians could also use such software to troubleshoot user problems with library applications.

But remote control software can be used for reference interaction and library instruction in addition to problem trouble shooting. The following example illustrates some of what can be done with reference service or library instruction using videoconferencing and remote application sharing software. NetMeeting is a free software program from Microsoft Corporation (1998) that includes both videoconferencing and remote application sharing features. It requires an Internet connection, the Windows95 or NT operating system, at least a 486 IBM compatible computer of at least 66 MHZ processing speed and at least 8 MB of RAM, but a Pentium processor with at least 12 MB of RAM is recommended (Microsoft Technical Support, 1997). A library with a web page states that for best distance reference service the user with a Windows95 or NT IBM PC that is equipped with a video camera can download and install NetMeeting to facilitate better distance reference service. The library web page would include a link to the Microsoft NetMeeting download site and another link to a copy of installation instructions for NetMeeting. The library also includes its reference telephone number to answer user questions about the installation and setup of NetMeeting. The library web page also states the hours when remote reference service is available and has a link to its computer station that runs NetMeeting so that once the user is setup he can easily start a NetMeeting session with the library.

The library has established a workstation with videoconferencing equipment and NetMeeting software at either the reference desk or the office of a reference librarian. At opening of the library this videoconferencing station is turned on and set to notify when an incoming videoconferencing call is received. A reference librarian accepting the incoming call activates NetMeeting and establishes a two way audio-video channel for videoconferencing with the user who is also using NetMeeting. The reference interview begins by video conference. For example, the librarian determines this first time remote user is not familiar with the library's online catalog, which is web based and also has a link from the library web page. To demonstrate the online catalog's use, the librarian starts his station's browser to the library's web page. Then in NetMeeting the librarian starts the "share" option which displays the open browser application to both the librarian and the user. The librarian can show the user how the online catalog works while he watches the application display on his screen and listens over the videoconferencing link. One of the features shown to the distant user would be the library's web based book or document delivery request form so the user can obtain the books that he had found in the online catalog. The requested books would be mailed to him as part of the library's distant user support services.

In another calling session a user might need instruction in the use of an online full text resource the library makes available to distant users. The librarian could start by "sharing" the application with the user to demonstrate it to him. After some instruction the user might have a question where it would be best for him to control the full text application. The librarian engages the NetMeeting "collaborate" feature and so does the user. This starts a two-way session where either party can control the application. Then the user manipulates the application while the librarian watches and advises the user on what to do. Control of the application can be passed back and forth as necessary.

NetMeeting also has a chat window and a shared whiteboard that can be used as tools in the reference interaction. The Window's clipboard is also shared by NetMeeting such that one person can "copy" to the clipboard and the other person "paste" from it to his computer desktop. This might be employed by a user to give his contact information to the reference librarian so the librarian could reply to him with the answer to his reference question. Additionally, NetMeeting has a file transfer function for copying files from the computer of one party to the computer of another such that the answer to the reference question might be transmitted by file transfer back to the user in another session.

NetMeeting and many other videoconferencing programs, such as the commercial White Pine version of CU-SeeMe, are now compliant with the H.323 standard for Internet video transmission. This enables users with different videoconferencing programs and even different computer platforms to have videoconferencing sessions. The commercial remote control application Timbuktu from Farallon Communications has versions that run on Macintosh, Windows 3.1, Windows95, Windows NT, and Unix computers. A library trying to accommodate users with more types of computers than Windows95 or Windows NT might use an H.323 compliant videoconferencing program and Timbuktu for remote application sharing so that they could interact with more types of computer users. But in this case the users would have to purchase and install a version of Timbuktu on their computer because for remote application sharing both parties must be using the same software as there is not a remote control software standard that allows inter-program operability.

These are just a few examples of what can be done at this time. The current status of the Internet with traffic jams and the telecommunications infrastructure with slow telephone lines to most locations, especially to those remote areas that need distant services the most, make desktop videoconferencing relatively primitive, with the ability to achieve even close to full motion video a rarity. The rapid evolution of computing and telecommunications will soon make the specific examples given in this article obsolete, but the principles of using some form of videoconferencing and remote application sharing in reference service will develop with the technology and communications infrastructure.

CONCLUSIONS

The paradigm of the library as a collection of books in a static place that the user must visit is rapidly changing to that of an institution that provides access to the information resources and materials that its users need from a variety of sources, not necessarily just their own physical collection. As demand for remote or distant provision of library services and functions like reference and library instruction become greater, librarians must employ computer tools like videoconferencing and remote application sharing to make them possible. Just as the paradigm of the library changes, the manner in which reference librarians operate will change. The added role of a remote expert who interacts by videoconferencing and using shared remote computer applications will come to pass.

REFERENCES

CU-SeeMe Development Team, Cornell University. "CU-SeeMe Welcome Page" Available URL: http://cu-seeme.cornell.edu/ Accessed on 6/15/1997.

Folger, Kathleen A. "The virtual librarian: Using desktop videoconferencing to provide interactive reference assistance." *ACRL 1997 National Conference Papers* Available URL: http://www.ala.org/acrl/paperhtm/a09.html Accessed on 3/15/1998.

Microsoft Corporation. "NetMeeting Quick Tutorial" Available URL: http://www.microsoft.com/netmeeting/demo/demo_plain.htm Accessed on 3/23/ 1998.

Microsoft Technical Support. "NetMeeting Readme Online, README for Microsoft NetMeeting 2.1 October 1997" Available URL: http://support.microsoft.com/support/netmeeting/readme/default.asp Accessed on 3/23/1998.

White Pine Software. "CU-SeeMe Read Me Version 3.1 for Windows 95 & NT 4.0" Available URL: http://www.cuseeme.com/cu31-win-readme.html Accessed on 1/24/98.

Reference and Media–
Instruction by Any Means Necessary

Necia Parker-Gibson

SUMMARY. Reference services involve using technologies to teach users how to locate and use needed resources. The use of various media for the presentation of library instruction has gone on since the 1930s. A chronology of the use of film, slides, audio tape, videotape, television, and computer-assisted instruction is presented here with brief commentary on the positive and negative aspects of the use of each type of technology and some combinations of technologies for instruction. *[Article copies available for a fee from The Haworth Document Delivery Service: 1-800-342-9678. E-mail address: getinfo@haworthpressinc.com]*

KEYWORDS. Reference services, library instruction, instructional media

The word *media* as it relates to reference work is used within two contexts:

1. answering questions and helping readers find various media for their use, i.e., videos, slides, movies, computer programs, computer-assisted instruction, and so on
2. using media tools for teaching readers how to use a particular library, department, collection or resource; such tools include audio-tapes, videotapes, presentation software, computer-assisted instruc-

Necia Parker-Gibson is Associate Librarian and Library Instruction Coordinator, Mullins Library, University of Arkansas, Fayetteville, AR 72701.

[Haworth co-indexing entry note]: "Reference and Media–Instruction by Any Means Necessary." Parker-Gibson, Necia. Co-published simultaneously in *The Reference Librarian* (The Haworth Information Press, an imprint of The Haworth Press, Inc.) No. 65, 1999, pp. 61-78; and: *Reference Services and Media* (ed: Martha Merrill) The Haworth Information Press, an imprint of The Haworth Press, Inc., 1999, pp. 61-78. Single or multiple copies of this article are available for a fee from The Haworth Document Delivery Service [1-800-342-9678, 9:00 a.m. - 5:00 p.m. (EST). E-mail address: getinfo@haworthpressinc. com].

61

tion (CAI), various forms of distance education and instruction via the Internet or some combination of these variations.

WHY USE MEDIA?

Although there are important points to be thought of and addressed in the first case, my focus will be the *second* facet, that of library or bibliographic instruction services via media since, particularly in academic libraries, instruction and orientation are usually considered a reference function.

Access to library collections is becoming more and more complex as libraries supplement their books, journals, print indexes and abstracts with resources in various electronic formats including databases accessed through the Internet and electronic full-text sources. Yet, adoption of technology by libraries, according to Harvey Sager, has made our teaching more acceptable to our patrons:

> It would not be an exaggeration to say that technology has validated BI as an essential library mission, and revolutionized the "what," the "way," and the "why" we think about, write about, and deliver bibliographic instruction to our user populations. (p. 51)[1]

While the author refers to "emerging technologies" such as computer databases, CD-ROMs, and so on–which to him require instruction because they differ both from the older forms of library resources and from each other and indicates that it is the technology that increases the need for and validates the instruction–I think that a reciprocal statement holds as well. Although the design, quality and content of instruction is most important, the presentation of library instruction through media seems to appeal to librarians and has a beneficial effect, at least in terms of public relations, on their patrons.[2] The presentation of instruction using visual, audible or interactive technology makes it appear less static and more attractive to the participants. In many cases, the *medium* of instruction may actually help validate or support it[3] especially as the students are increasingly of the television, video, and computer-using generations. In Eric Rumsey's study, when the students evaluated the qualitative experience of the instruction, the HyperCard tutorial was preferred over handouts or other materials even though the content was similar.[4]

WHEN AND WHY WE PREFER TO USE MEDIA FOR LIBRARY INSTRUCTION

As soon as a form of instructional media comes into a reasonable (i.e., economical) price range and availability, it is likely to be examined and if found potentially useful, to be adopted by librarians for instruction. The reasons for this are many, but I would mention three. First, there are always more students in need of general, basic instruction than we can reach in lecture or demonstration classes or face-to-face at the Reference desk. Second, printed materials such as workbooks or manuals are expensive, time-consuming to grade and edit, and sometimes not well liked by students forcing librarians to seek alternatives. Third, teaching many classes in the basic forms of research instruction repeatedly in the same way can cause librarians to suffer fatigue and possible loss of interest and morale. Developing other forms of instruction may be done to save time, both for students and librarians, to provide consistent instruction to many on a flexible schedule and to reduce stress.[5]

AN EXAMINATION OF THE LITERATURE: IN THE BEGINNING, FILMS!

I have briefly examined *Library Literature* from the 1921-1932 volume to the current year. Although the history of library instruction begins much earlier,[6] the earliest *mention* I have found of the use of a form of media for library instruction is in 1932, with the mention of instruction apparently *by radio* in an article by M. T. Hugentugler[7] and then by film in an article by M. A. Downing in the same year.[8] The next step, a generalized film produced for the library market, came in 1936 with the release of "Found in a Book" produced by the University of Illinois Library School.[9] In parallel with the development of films as an instructional medium, the use of manuals, workbooks, programmed texts, and written self-paced tours appears in the index. Since it is well covered in the literature, the use of workbooks and manuals will only be touched upon peripherally here.

Films were (and sometimes are) a popular form of library instruction although many of them have titles which suggest that they are intended more to relieve library anxiety than to teach.[10] However, they share certain problems with many later media formats, including videotapes and computer-assisted instruction, such as:

1. high initial cost for the design, development and production of a "work," including the necessary time, technology and expertise, whether hired or in-house
2. limited application of the developed item to other libraries
3. a large time commitment for editing and updating[11]
4. the fact that a bad media product is worse than none[12]
5. evaluation of the provided instruction is necessary but not always as easy to accomplish as with workbooks or posttests
6. late adoption of a technology or format may make it outdated too soon in the life of the product to make it cost-effective, which is difficult to forecast–i.e., microprint, beta videotapes or some types of software.

FILM STRIPS AND SLIDES

Film strips and slides were adopted for library instruction beginning in the 1930s and continued from that time. The earliest mention of slide-based tours in *Library Literature* is in 1932,[13] and many librarians' earliest professional exposure to the use of media for teaching came in the form of development and use of slide tours for bibliographic instruction or library orientation. Slide tours or instruction sets were clearly preferred to film strips because they were so much easier to revise.[14] Speculation was made during these years on at least one campus about whether "instruction in library use" could be turned over to technology entirely since Paul Wendt found no difference between the test results of lecture-trained students and "teaching-machine" taught students; the medium in this case was slides with illustrative photographs on one side and text on the other.[15] Most early slide tours had printed instruction on the slides or were accompanied by a lecture, a notebook, or manual. Recorded commentary came later starting with phonograph records and then tape recordings. Slide presentations for instruction, rather than orientation, were more likely to be associated with a lecture or demonstration than a recording unless the instruction was self-paced. Instruction by slide set might cover a single reference tool–particularly for point-of-use instruction (commonly, how to use the card catalog or *Readers' Guide*)–or focus on the use of several tools, or be a general overview of how to use a particular library.

TELEVISION

In the 1950s and 1960s, media-based instruction by slide, filmstrip, and film was joined by television presentations.[16] Instruction by television was not noted heavily in the literature; closed circuit television was the most prevalent early use. The medium of television was not well suited for some types of instruction. For example, showing someone how to use a reference book or to look at entries in an index over a small screen was difficult since there was no magnification by projection and since the technology for either live or prerecorded television was expensive.

AUDIO TAPES

References to articles about audio taped library instruction begin to appear in the 1970s[17] and recur periodically from that time. Although slide tours have given way in many cases to other kinds of presentations, audio taped tours are still in use in some libraries.[18] In fact, some libraries continue to use slides and audiotapes in combination,[19] a procedure which was common beginning in the 1970s. Larry L. Hardesty (1978) detailed the results of a survey which measured the cost, time needed to produce, and use of such presentations in academic libraries.[20] *Educating the Library User*, edited by John Lubans, covers many facets of library instruction in the decade[21] and has selections detailing the use of audiovisual materials for instruction; slide/tape presentations are featured in several. The technology may have changed; for example, the "slides" may be computer-generated or augmented graphics rather than photographic slides. Many of the issues remain, such as the level of expertise needed to design and create the program, how to engage the students in the instruction, how to make sure that the machines work as they should and when they should, and how to evaluate the instruction.

A comparison study was done in 1973 by Frank F. Kuo.[22] Kuo compared the results of different kinds of instruction (lecture with provided notebooks, audio taped presentation without visual instruction, slide/audiotape with timed forwarding, television instruction [self-paced presentation made from the slides, on a TV screen, with audio taped narration and notebook] and self-paced slide/audiotape with notebook and follow-up by the librarians). Apparently, all students with library instruction of some kind did better on a related post-test than the control group; the self-paced instruction with slides with audiotape and librarian follow-up did best, as one might expect, although that structure, if adopted, would offset a common intention of instruction via media: letting the librarians do something above and beyond repetitive general instruction.

The effectiveness of self-paced audio taped tours is mixed according to the survey by Lorna Peterson,[23] but the most effective use was in conjunction with an integrated course of library instruction. She mentions that, logically enough, most of the audio taped tours are used in large academic libraries on campuses with many students. These tours often serve to familiarize the students with the building or buildings and with library services. Some libraries currently have a total instruction set which includes an audio taped tour, a handbook with exercises, demonstrations, and printed pathfinders and quizzes.[24] Some libraries use audio taped tours or presentations with slides and an audio taped narration with apparent commitment and pleasure.[25] The use of audio taped tours or instruction continues for several reasons. It is inexpensive to make multiple copies of the tapes once they are completed. Tape players have been made progressively smaller and less expensive since their common adoption in the 1970s. Thus, with multiple tapes and players, libraries can provide many students with a self-paced tour simultaneously. Tape players can be used easily by most people with little training, and the tours can be taken at any time that the library is open. The combination of listening to instruction and seeing the points of interest is useful for some learners because the tapes are self-paced and segments or even the whole tour can be repeated if needed. The drawbacks are that the initial tape may be costly in time and effort to produce in good quality and to edit or revise; the instruction may not engage the students; and the amount of use of the tours varies from high to almost nil, depending largely on whether or not the tours are required for a particular course or class assignment.

Patricia Senn Breivik in *Planning the Library Instruction Pro-*

gram[26] questions the value of tours by whatever medium. She details the possible choices for instruction with a chart of potential attributes of each kind of instruction (such as people-oriented, resembles real-life situations, flexibility in learning or pace, requires active involvement of learner, and so on), showing, by +, 1/2, or 0, how much benefit a type of instruction provides. In her opinion, guided tours score in none of the positive areas, and self-paced tours only score under flexibility. Computer-assisted instruction, course-integrated instruction, credit courses, and combinations of instruction scored highest (p. 70). Motivation is a key factor to Breivik, and she questions whether any form of instruction will be effective without some relation to course work or other consequences.

Peterson mentions the relative ineffectiveness of guided tours in contrast with audio taped tours.[27] The guided tours tended to be less consistent in their content and not always at the best pace for an individual student. She found few articles actually evaluated, rather than simply described, a given library's guided tours and mentioned that Piette and Dance,[28] who did ask for evaluation, found 55 percent of the graduate students in their study thought the guided tours were less than helpful.

VIDEOTAPES

The first mention of videotape for instruction appears in the literature in 1970,[29] and it becomes more popular in the literature through the 1980s. However, the drawbacks are similar to those of film: the production of videotapes is expensive especially if it involves hired expertise, and in-house productions may come across to the viewers as cheap and amateurish. As with films, videotapes become out of date quickly especially if they are used to demonstrate computer-based catalogs or databases. In addition, it is quite possible to try to cover too much material in a videotape just as it is with any other type of instruction. Breivik (1982) also discusses the use of films and videos for instruction. While videotapes and films have their place, she felt:

> In general, the best use of AV productions for group viewing is for general orientation and building positive attitudes towards the library. Stressing the importance of information in today's society, describing the ways in which libraries serve to make infor-

mation available, or giving a brief introduction to a particular library or library service may offer appropriate focuses. The section on tours has noted the inherent dangers of including too much detailed information in such orientations. Concerns about production quality are even more serious in group AV presentations than point of use since the potential for affecting attitudes is so great. Moreover, the larger screen makes mistakes and lack of quality all the more noticeable, not to mention the mounting negative effect that disenchanted or amused audience reactions can have. For these reasons, ongoing user evaluation and frequent updating are crucial. (p. 78)[30]

So, it is clear that videotapes can be used to introduce students to a particular library, to reduce anxiety, to give viewers an idea of location of services and materials, or in some cases, to teach one specific tool or database as with the videotapes available about *PsycLit*.

Commercially produced videotapes are used by libraries in some circumstances but are regarded by many as less effective than materials tailored to a particular library or context. An unusual and interesting blend of video-based instruction with a workshop or seminar was developed recently by BYU,[31] where the librarians first show a video. Then, they stop the film to talk about library anxiety, to discuss how to use the sources illustrated by the video, and to answer questions. This prize-winning video cost about $40,000 to shoot and used student actors and on-campus media services to film it. BYU also requires their students to use a taped tour of the library, a computer-assisted instruction module, and a programmed text with exercises. Their dedication to library instruction is clear!

COMPUTER-ASSISTED INSTRUCTION

Mention of computer-assisted instruction begins to appear in the mid-1960s under the term "programmed instruction,"[32] and evaluation of it begins in the early 1970s.[33] The earliest uses of it appear to be for training librarians and library staff.[34] It is more commonly mentioned in the context of science, medical, or other special libraries than more general types of libraries. As the hardware and software got less expensive and more readily available and as programming expertise spread in the library population, more libraries adopted the use of

CAI. The development and use of CAI has continued although, as with other forms of media instruction, it is not cheap. The computer(s) and software may be a special purchase, and the development cost in time is often in the hundreds of hours. The projected amount of use of the program must be considered, for if the users are few, it is likely to be more economical to use either one-on-one instruction at the Reference desk or consultations by appointment. Although software editors for HTML and other languages have made construction of some instruction modules much simpler, CAI still suffers from the problem of being time intensive in development and has the potential for being technologically marooned as the hardware or software changes.

In addition, a delicate line must be drawn between providing a level of instruction too elementary or too complicated; the audience for the program, the time and way they are likely to use it, and the number of terminals that will carry it are all considerations. Many instruction modules are progressive from providing the most general to focusing on the most specific information or are menu-driven so that users may choose their own level or type of instruction. Although commercial products, such as *Research Assistant* created by Ann Bevilacqua,[35] have been available and some of these programs may be modified or tailored to the particular library and resources available, the trend has been to create library-specific or resource-specific instruction within a library to address a specific population and their needs.

Many CAI programs were started on Apple computers using versions of HyperCard[36] because the Apple had a graphical user interface (GUI) and good graphics capability and because the programming languages HyperTalk and HyperScript were relatively simple to learn and use. The HyperCard software was inexpensive and later came bundled with the computer. HyperCard has been remarkable in its longevity and number of users because of these qualities. The earliest mention of HyperCard in the literature is in 1988,[37] and the most recent citation is in 1996.[38] It has been used for CAI in almost every kind of library, from school libraries to university libraries.

Programs such as ToolBook,[39] which was a PC-clone version of a program similar to HyperCard, allowed non-Macintosh users to develop CAI. As the computer market expanded and the possibilities of computer networks grew, and especially as programs which could be read across various computer platforms became popular, the potential for CAI expanded with it. The rise of languages such as HTML,

SGML, Perl, Java, and others has meant that more machines can read more software than at any previous time, and more librarians can design and write software than ever. The newest versions of CAI, mounted on the World Wide Web (WWW), are available regardless of platform if the reader has a computer with a browser.[40] Although the first tutorials over campus networks or the Internet were text-based, improvements in connections to networks, servers, and clients have allowed the potential for a full range of multimedia instruction. If a computer is equipped with the correct hardware and software, the user can see text and images, hear cues or instructions or music, receive context-specific tutoring, and watch video clips. However, the hardware and software of the likely users, on- and off-campus, must be considered. It does little good to have wonderful animation to illustrate a module if the average users have computers that do not support it.

At the same time, the ability to access library catalogs, databases, and other information through the campus network or through the Internet means that it is likely that more "virtual" (and thus invisible) users than ever are tapping into the resources without ever having had instruction. This may be another reason to mount CAI on a network. Although it is always a question whether or not the invisible patrons will use it, logs of IP addresses, if kept and examined, may reveal contact just as counter software will display "hits," if not use.

CAI programs, just as slide, film, or video instruction programs, are often evaluated against more traditional modes of instruction such as workbooks[41] or lectures and are considered successful if post-tests reveal retention and understanding similar to that of the other participants. A benefit of this type of instruction, particularly if it is available on networked computers or on the Internet, is the potential for increasing retention of material by review. Retention of instruction material is always an issue regardless of format; as Claire Weinstein has said, the forgetting curve is often as steep as the learning curve.[42] This kind of instruction is one way to provide unobtrusive review twenty-four hours a day. In many cases, it will not matter whether the students are on campus or what time they access the program.

The need to update and edit a CAI program may be frequent especially if modules are provided that teach specific tools and, in particular, if the resources are also computer-based. My own experience, not entirely unique, may illustrate the point. I started to build a CAI program with HyperCard, called "InfoThink," beginning in 1993.

Hundreds of hours later, I had developed a system of stacks which provided a virtual guided tour of the library, that described how to use the online catalog, showed how to use various indexes and how to find a particular periodical in our library, included a glossary of library terms which were hyperlinked in the text itself, and quizzed students on their knowledge at the end, returning them to the question if they made a mistake. It was mounted on the one Macintosh machine in the library and twenty-five machines in the University's Macintosh lab. It was evaluated by quiz results and surveys of students and some faculty as being just as if not more useful than the standard lecture instruction. I provided two major revisions of the program because of changes in the online catalog and available databases and added more subject-specific lists of sources. About two years after the program was mounted on the machines in the University lab, the software in the lab was changed by campus Computing Services making the copies un-readable. I attempted at that time to translate the HyperCard program software directly into HTML code, but it proved impossible. In the end, I used the InfoThink program as a mental template for the development of a similar program written in HTML code, which has proved to be more stable and because of the Internet, more available across campus. The new program, called "Jumpstart," is a Web-mounted instruction module. We have used it to orient off-campus students such as the local high school groups and for initial training of student assistants.

OTHER TECHNOLOGIES, OTHER COMBINATIONS

During the 1980s and 1990s the use of photographic slides plus lecture, audio taped instruction tours, videotaped instruction, and other methods continued. In addition, many libraries began to offer lectures as well as live demonstrations of databases or the online catalog, often using a computer, a CD-ROM, and an LCD panel or other projection medium.[43,44] As campuses became more consistently networked, computer-generated software presentations with projected demonstrations were provided using live access to networked or Web-based modules or resources when and where possible and software presentations with captured screens for canned presentations when network access is limited or slow. Important software programs for computer-generated presentations include PowerPoint, Harvard Graphics, Word-

Perfect Presentations, and others.[45] In addition, as computers became more often available in greater numbers, many library instruction classrooms have become labs where demonstrations are followed by hands-on practice by individuals or groups.[46] The trend toward collaborative learning or instruction increases this practice. The next generation of computer-assisted instruction known as *Interactive Learning Environments* (ILEs) is available for the sciences and mathematics,[47] and it is likely to be only a matter of time (and money and programming) before library instruction can be delivered in this mode; some of the models for the other disciplines mentioned are collaborative–the results are constructed by student teams; some programs allow the results, ranging from reports to robots, to be based on the work of individual students. I suspect that the results or product from such a program if it were built for libraries would include a paper or speech outline with a list of sources.

DISTANCE EDUCATION

Library instruction as a form of distance education has been developed using many types of media. The most common form is by videotape, but it is also provided through compressed video signals transmitted along telephone networks to local computers and projectors or televisions, offered by traveling librarians using lecture and demonstration, and provided by computer-assisted instruction.[48] The common forms of television or video-based distance education are in connection with course-integrated library instruction and go out to satellite campuses.[49] In a sense, Internet or Web-based CAI may be considered a universal type of distance education since it can be accessed anywhere that a terminal with the right connections and software is available. Again, the needs of the students and the technology available to them must be considered if distance education is to be useful.

PREVIEWING A TYPE OF PRESENTATION

Various types of media often now tend to merge within one presentation: presentation software makes "slides;" videotapes can be translated into video clips on a computer; screen captures from a computer can be transferred onto videotape; photographs and slides can be digitized for computer graphics or transferred to videotape; and digital cameras provide images also usable by computers or able to be translated into photos or slides. Graphics software allows manipulation of almost all these types of images. The total picture of how to present instruction may not be as clear as it was in the past. There are ways to bring it into focus.

The Library Orientation Exchange (LOEX) was established in 1972 at Eastern Michigan University. LOEX sponsors a conference every spring where library instruction methods and theories are presented. In addition, it functions as a clearinghouse for library instruction materials and presentations. Librarians from all over the country donate copies of their work, and there are examples of most kinds of library instruction materials in the LOEX archives. Often, it is possible to borrow a copy of a video, slide set, or CAI program to look at and consider as an alternative for a local situation or even to use as a template with proper credit to the authors. Having the collection available allows for what may be its most valuable feature. If libraries can decide in favor of or against a given form of media for teaching library instruction without having to purchase the technology, produce the product, and then abandon it if it turns out to be inappropriate, this clearinghouse has saved the profession countless hours of work and frustration.

WHAT TO DO? HOW TO DECIDE?

The developments in technology and the blending of options make decisions concerning the type of media most appropriate for library instruction in individual libraries much more challenging. Use assessments, surveys, or other evaluations of need may be necessary. Linda Brew MacDonald, quoting Clark and Saloman,[50] tells us:

1. Past research on media has shown quite clearly that no medium enhances learning more that any other medium regardless of learning task, learner traits, symbolic elements, curriculum content or setting.

2. Any new technology is likely to teach better than its predecessors because it generally provides better prepared instructional materials and its novelty engages learners. (p. 30)

Although these statements are in some ways contradictory, the implication is that whatever we choose, if done well, should suffice and that the new technologies do seem more attractive to learners. She recommends that such choices about technology be based on a deliberate plan of instructional development and what Svinicki and Schwartz[51] refer to as "learner-control centered design." Needs assessment, analysis of tasks, development of instructional objectives, and the intention of making the instruction available to those who need it in an appropriately use-driven form are the keynotes of what she believes will be successful media-based instruction.

The content and pace of a videotape are relatively fixed and linear, and points may not be absorbed if the presentation is not self-paced. An audio tape session may not appeal to visual learners. A CAI program may allow so many choices that a student may not know where to start. If a library focuses effort solely on CAI, the computer-phobic students will either be left out of or less likely to be fully engaged in the instruction. A library that devotes its resources, time and librarians to lectures and demonstrations will need more staff and support than those that primarily use other means for basic instruction. A library without signs may cause frustration; a library with too many signs may cause confusion. No one form of instruction is going to benefit all users. No one form of instruction is going to be appropriate for all libraries. No form of media is universally ideal. Media for instruction is helpful, but it is only a set of tools. As Margaret W. Gordon says:

> Adherence to the lessons learned from the older, well-tested audiovisual technologies can carry the new ones to an exciting and effective level. The innovations are so appealing, in fact, that it is all too easy to lose sight of the two most important factors in library instruction: the people we need to teach and the information we want to teach them. We must see to it that the innovations themselves, however new and exciting, are not the focus of our efforts. (p. 174)[52]

Regardless of the presentation medium, instruction should demonstrate or teach how to use the most common resources or tools. What is taught should be clear. The amount of material should be appropriate for the time allotted and the type of instruction provided. Whether the instruction is developed by reference librarians or personnel in a separate department, the experience of librarians at the reference desk should be considered, and librarians should be consulted as instruction is developed. Instruction should focus on tools or materials that generate questions or problems for the local population of users as well as research concepts. Judah L. Schwartz, in an article discussing the use of CAI for teaching physics, speaks of the students' dismay when they discover that what they thought was scientific truth was only the best scientific *model* of a particular phenomena.[53] Although research is in many ways an art rather than a science, we need to show the students the most robust model of the best research practice that we have found. Ideally, media-based instruction should be available as a part of a reference referral so that librarians at the desk can show it to or recommend it to students as needed. This is easy with networked CAI, for example, but can also be accomplished with other forms. The reference librarians, whether they regularly teach basic instruction or not, should be able to count on the fact that most students of a certain level will at least have been exposed to the mechanics of the routine tasks of seeking and finding appropriate material in the library. In addition, enough detail should be provided in the instruction about library services so that the students and the librarians alike know what they can expect from each other when engaging in any reference interview or interaction. The instruction should be appealing, timely, useful and current. The intention, design and development must be right for the situation; if they are, good planning and implementation should yield good results.

REFERENCES

1. Sager, Harvey. (1995) Implications for Bibliographic Instruction. In *The Impact of Emerging Technologies on Reference Service and Bibliographic Instruction.* Gary Pitkin, ed. Contributions in Library and Information Science, number 87. Westport, CT: Greenwood Press.

2. Cooper, E.W. (1953) Use of Visual Media for Better Public Relations in a Medical Library. *Medical Library Association Bulletin.* 41:215-19.

3. Lolley, J.L. and R. Watkins. (1979) Use of Audiovisuals in Developing Favorable Attitudes Toward Library Instruction. *Educational Technology* 19: 56-8.

4. Rumsey, Eric. (1992) HyperCard for Bibliographic Instruction. *Computers in Libraries* 12 (5): 43-5.

5. Dixon, Lana, Marie Garrett, Rita Smith and Alan Wallace. (1995) Build Library Skills: Computer-Assisted Instruction for Undergraduates. *Research Strategies* 13 (4): 196-208, for one detailed example of the progression.

6. Tiefel, Virginia May. (1995) Library User Education: Examining Its Past, Projecting Its Future. (Gateway to Information, developed by the Ohio State University library). *Library Trends* 44: 318-38.

7. Hugentugler, M.T. (1932) Library Instruction by Radio. *Library Journal*. 57: 185.

8. Downing, M.A. (1932) Library Instruction by Film. *Library Journal* 57: 132.

9. *ALA Bulletin* (September 1936) 30: 899.

10. Shain, Charles H. (1976) Filming Narrative for Library Instruction Film *You Don't Have to be a Hero to Use the U. C. Library*. Berkeley: University of California. ERIC Document ED 134215.

11. Peterson, Lorna. (1996) A Survey of U.S. Libraries on the Use of Audiotape Orientation Tours. *Research Strategies* 14 (1): 22-35.

12. Hardesty, Larry L. (1977) Use of Slide/Tape Presentations in Academic Libraries: A State-of-the-Art Survey. *Journal of Academic Librarianship* 3: 137-40.

13. Keith, Mrs. R. (1932) Visual Methods of Library Instruction. *Wilson Bulletin* 6: 694-700, and Bennett, M.A.(1938) Microfilm and its Use in Giving Instruction in the Use of the Library. *Special Library Association Proceedings* 1: 97-8.

14. Smith, X.P. (1940) Visualizing Library Instruction. *Wilson Library Bulletin* 15: 247-8.

15. Wendt, Paul and others. (1963) Study to Determine The Extent to Which Instruction to University Freshmen in the Use of the University Library Can Be Turned Over to Teaching Machines: Final Report. Carbondale, IL: Southern Illinois University. ERIC Document ED 003559.

16. Bolander, L.H. (1955) TV Classroom on Library Techniques. *Library Journal* 80: 2471-2. and McComb, R.W. (1958) Closed Circuit Television in a Library Orientation Program. *College and Research Libraries* 19: 358-9.

17. Peterman, Edward and Jim Holsclaw. (1971) Library Orientation in a New Mode. *Audiovisual Instruction* 16 (2): 46-7.

18. Peterson, 1996.

19. Du Mont, Mary J. and Barbara F. Schloman. (1995) The Evolution and Reaffirmation of a Library Orientation Program in an Academic Research Library (from lecture tour to self-guided audiotape tour at Kent State University). *Reference Services Review* 23 (1): 85-92.

20. Hardesty, Larry L. 1978. *Use of Slide/tape Presentations in Academic Libraries :[with a] special section, "Sound/slide Presentations: Six Faults"* by John Murphy. New York: J. Norton Publishers. Also, seven out of twelve articles indexed in 1978 under audio-visual materials are about slide/tape combinations, and this proportion increases in 1979 and 1980.

21. Lubans, John, ed. 1974. *Educating the Library User.* New York: R.R. Bowker Co.

22. Kuo, Frank F. (1973) A Comparison of Six Versions of Science Library Instruction. *College and University Libraries* 34 (3): 287-290.

23. Peterson, 1996.

24. Willis, Elizabeth I. and Diane J. Turner. (1995) Streamlining Library Instruction: the Auraria Experience. *Research Strategies* 13 (2): 107-115.

25. Du Mont and Schloman, 1995. and Rogers, Steven E.; James R. Nance; Linda K. Butler. (1993) Slide/tape Presentations: Cost-effective Library Instruction. *Research Strategies* 11 (1): 4-8.

26. Breivik, Patricia Senn. 1982. *Planning the Library Instruction Program*. Chicago: American Library Association, 1982. p. 70.

27. Peterson, 1996.

28. Piette, Mary I. and Betty Dance. (1993) A Statistical Evaluation of a Library Orientation Program for Graduate Students. *Research Strategies* 11 (2): 164-173.

29. Wyatt, R.W.P. Production of Video-tapes For Library Instruction: an Account of Experience at Brunel University. IN *Educating the Library User*, p L1-5; Conference proceedings, International Association of Technological University Libraries, Loughbourough: England, 1970.

30. Breivik. 1982, p. 78.

31. Tidwell, Sandra L. (1994). Reducing Library Anxiety with a Creative Video and In-class Discussion. *Research Strategies* 12 (3): 187-90.

32. Jernigan, E.T. (1967) Computer-assisted Instruction for Library Processes. *Special Libraries* 58: 631-3.

33. Hansen, L.N. (1972) Computer-assisted Instruction in Library Use: An Evaluation. *Drexel Library Quarterly* 8: 345-55.

34. For example, Starks, D.D. (1972) Two Modes of Computer-Assisted Instruction in a Library Reference Course. *Journal of the American Society for Information Science* 23: 271-7.

35. Bevilacqua, Ann F. 1993. Research Assistant (for library instruction). In *Bibliographic Instruction in Practice: a Tribute to Evan Ira Farber*. Ann Arbor, Mich.: Pierian Press.

36. Vander Meer, Patricia and Galen E. Rike. (1995) Multimedia: Meeting the Demand for User Education with a Self-Instructional Tutorial. *Research Strategies* 14 (3): 145-158, and Kesselman, Martin A. (1988) LSM Infomaster: a HyperCard CAI program on a Macintosh Network. *College & Research Libraries News* 49 (7): 437-40.

37. Cisler, Steve. (1988) HyperCard: Software for the Macintosh. *Small Computers in Libraries* 8: 26-9.

38. Kiyabu, Katherine. (1996) Hawaii with HyperCard. *The School Librarian's Workshop* 16: 5.

39. Nance, William D. (1991) ToolBook from Asymetrix: User-oriented Application Development Software. *CD-ROM Professional* 4: 50-4.

40. For example, see Schwartz, Kathryn. "A+ Research and Writing, Step by Step."(1997) at http://www.ipl.org/teen/aplus/stepfirst.htm (05/21/98), or my own "Jumpstart!"(1997) at http://www.uark.edu/libinfo/refdept/instruction (05/21/98).

41. Vander Meer, 1995.

42. Weinstein, Claire. (1992) Address at LOEX Conference. *What is Good Instruction Now? Library Instruction for the 90's*. The Twentieth National LOEX Library Instruction Conference. May 1992. Linda Shirato, ed. Ann Arbor, Michigan:

Published for Learning Resources and Technologies, Eastern Michigan University, by Pierian Press, 1993.

43. Saule, Mara R. (1991) Teaching for Library Technologies. In *Teaching Technologies in Libraries: A Practical Guide.* Linda Brew MacDonald et al., p. 1-28. Boston: G.K. Hall & Co.

44. Parker-Gibson, Necia. (1994) Taking It to the Streets: Mobile CD-ROM Workshops on Campus (at the University of Arkansas, Fayetteville). *Research Strategies* 12 (3): 122-6.

45. Tripp, Peter. (1997) Presentation power (rating PowerPoint 7.0, Harvard Graphics 4.0, Freelance Graphics 96, Astound 4.0, Director 5.0). *Library Journal.* 122: 42-3.

46. Hanson, Michele G. Joining the Conversation: Collaborative Learning and Bibliographic Instruction. In *Library Instruction Revisited: Bibliographic Instruction Comes of Age.* Lynne M. Martin, ed. New York: The Haworth Press, Inc., 1995. The archives of *BI-L*, a library instruction discussion list, bear this out.

47. Solloway, Elliot. (1991). Quick, Where Do the Computers Go? *Communications of the ACM* 34 (2): 29-33.

48. Slade, Alexander L. and Marie A. Kascus. 1996. *Library Services for Off-Campus and Distance Education: the Second Annotated Bibliography.* Englewood, Colorado: Libraries Unlimited, Inc.

49. Conversation with Elizabeth C. McKee, education librarian, 4/5/98.

50. Clark, Richard and Gavriel Saloman. (1985) Media in Teaching. In *Handbook of Research on Teaching*, Merlin Wittrock, ed. p. 464-75. New York: Macmillan. Quoted in: MacDonald, Linda Brew. (1991) Deciding Among the Options. IN *Teaching Technologies in Libraries: A Practical Guide.* MacDonald et al., eds. Boston: G.K. Hall & Co.

51. Svinicki, Marilla and Barbara Schwartz. (1988) *Designing Instruction for Library Users: A Practical Guide.* New York: Dekker. Quoted in: MacDonald, Linda Brew. (1991) Deciding Among the Options. In *Teaching Technologies in Libraries: A Practical Guide.* MacDonald et al., eds. Boston: G.K. Hall & Co.

52. Gordon, Margaret W. (1991) The Audiovisual Renaissance. In *Teaching Technologies in Libraries: A Practical Guide.* MacDonald et al., eds. Boston: G.K. Hall & Co.

53. Schwartz, Judah. (1996) Motion Toys for Eye and Mind. *Communications of the ACM* 39 (8): 94-96.

Using Creativity:
Creating a Hands-On Learning Environment in Times of Tight Budgets

Gail M. Staines
John Craig

SUMMARY. The purpose of this article is to provide readers with creative methods for procuring funding for building an electronic information literacy instruction classroom. Using the Library Instruction Program at Niagara County Community College as a case study, the authors explain how grant funding was obtained to create a 24-computer lab classroom to teach students how to search for information effectively. A complete explanation of instruction provided to grant participants is also included. This article is particularly useful for librarians working with limited resources and for instruction librarians responsible for teaching students how to search for information in electronic form effectively. *[Article copies available for a fee from The Haworth Document Delivery Service: 1-800-342-9678. E-mail address: getinfo@haworthpressinc.com]*

KEYWORDS. Reference service, library instruction, funding

Reference service in libraries has traditionally included instruction. Whether instruction is one-on-one with a patron or in groups, teaching

---

Gail M. Staines is Executive Director, WNY Library Resources Council, 4455 Genesee St., P.O. Box 400, Buffalo, NY 14225-0400. John Craig is Director of Niagara County Tech Prep Consortium, Niagara County Community College, 3111 Saunders Settlement Rd., Sanborn, NY 14132.

[Haworth co-indexing entry note]: "Using Creativity: Creating a Hands-On Learning Environment in Times of Tight Budgets." Staines, Gail M., and John Craig. Co-published simultaneously in *The Reference Librarian* (The Haworth Information Press, an imprint of The Haworth Press, Inc.) No. 65, 1999, pp. 79-88; and: *Reference Services and Media* (ed: Martha Merrill) The Haworth Information Press, an imprint of The Haworth Press, Inc., 1999, pp. 79-88. Single or multiple copies of this article are available for a fee from The Haworth Document Delivery Service [1-800-342-9678, 9:00 a.m. - 5:00 p.m. (EST). E-mail address: getinfo@haworthpressinc.com].

people how to search for information effectively is a role prominent in reference. With the increase in use of all forms of media to locate information (Internet, CD-ROMs, multimedia, laser disks, etc.) comes the demand on the part of patrons to wanting to learn how to search different sources effectively to locate information. The need to learn how to search effectively for information is particularly evident when using various electronic sources where no standardization in user interfaces exists.

Library instruction librarians have been keen over the years in identifying the best methods to teach library users how to locate information. Beginning with the library tour and orientation, information literacy programs have evolved into teaching students how to create a search strategy, the best sources to use to locate information, and how to evaluate information for authoritativeness, reliability, and credibility. Many libraries have moved forward, establishing electronic classrooms to provide students with a hands-on learning environment. Libraries with limited resources continue to teach students how to search electronic sources by demonstration.

This article will provide readers with a creative process for procuring funding for building an electronic information literacy instruction classroom. Using the Library Instruction Program at Niagara County Community College as a case study, the process of obtaining grant funding will be explained. A complete explanation of instruction provided to grant participants is also included.

IMPORTANCE OF THE ISSUE

One might ask why the need for creating an electronic environment to teach in is so important. Clearly, the answer lies in the goals of instruction: that of teaching students to search for information effectively and in student retention of learning concepts and skills. Seeking an answer to this question can be placed into perspective by looking at the ways in which librarians have traditionally taught information seeking skills. It can also be found in reviewing proven retention methods of instruction.

Library instruction, library user education, bibliographic instruction, library orientation, information literacy–whatever term is used to describe the teaching and learning process of how to access information effectively–has a rich historical past. For over one hundred years, librarians have been teaching library users how to access information. Initially, library instruction began as book talks, lectures, and tours. This expanded to incorporating a wide variety of audio-visual materials into instruction. Computer assisted instruction, pathfinders, point-of-use materials, reference consultations, self-guided tours, term paper clinics, and credit bearing courses were designed to meet student learning needs.[1] Today, library instruction librarians are creating web-based information literacy courses for credit and for use as tutorials via the Internet. A shift has occurred from showing library users the physical location of materials to teaching concepts, critical thinking, and adaptable skills, both on campus and through distance learning initiatives.

The methods of teaching library users how to search for information effectively has also evolved. In the early years of instruction, librarians gave the traditional library tour–walking students around the library and pointing to important resources and services. Library orientations were then designed to give instruction on the use of library catalogs and indexes. Done by demonstration, students were shown how to search for a book and locate a periodical article. Active learning techniques were introduced with hands-on activities and group work. Librarians and faculty gave performance tasks for students to complete after demonstration of the source was given. With the introduction of technology into library and information science, such as the automation of online catalogs, students were again shown how to access information. Many libraries have now created a library instruction computer lab. This aids in teaching as students can watch a demonstration and then conduct an actual search upon immediately receiving instruction.

Electronic classrooms are an important step in improving student retention of skills and concepts. As Dale's learning pyramid illustrates, students retain 5% of information presented by lecture, 10% by reading, 20% by watching an audio-visual presentation, 30% by demonstration, 50% by participating in a discussion group, 75% by practicing, and 90% by teaching others.[2] Building an electronic library instruction classroom and providing students with a hands-on learning environment and an opportunity to share learning experiences improves retention.

PROCURING FUNDING

Our problem was identified. We needed to build a library instruction electronic classroom to provide our students with a hands-on learning environment. Funding needed to be procured for this venture. A traditional approach to locating funding sources was begun. Reference sources which listed possible funding agencies were searched. These included *The Grants Register* and the *Annual Register of Grant Support*. The World Wide Web was also searched for possibilities including the *Foundation Center* web site and *IAN Web Resources*.[3] Agency and corporate programs which met the criteria for funding our project were selected. The college grants officer made preliminary inquiries to possible funding sources selected. Institutions whose funding criteria had changed or who were not interested in funding our project were deselected from our list of possibilities.

It was becoming clear through this process that the funding sources being selected as possibilities were also highly competitive. Chances of receiving funding for such a small project were slim. We needed to rethink our approach and began to look in our own backyard to see what grant proposals were being prepared by other individuals at the college. Our thinking was that if we could dovetail our project with another project being pursued on campus, our proposal would be strengthened and our chances for receiving funding would improve. Through this search of proposals, the grant being written for Tech Prep funding came to our attention.

TECH PREP

Tech Prep is an educational program offered in high school which provides "hands-on" learning experiences for students who have an interest in the following career fields: Engineering Technology, Business/Office Technology, and Allied Health. Carl D. Perkins VATEA funds sponsored by the federal government and administered through the New York State Education Department support Tech Prep.[4] For the last four years, local area high schools and Niagara County Community College have worked to develop a program of study that meets the expectations in both the high school and post-secondary environments. This work has generated a "seamless" or non-repetitive curriculum whereby students are educated in the necessary areas to ensure future school and employment success.

The Tech Prep program provides realistic opportunities in learning situations which are non-traditionally based. This means that classes are taught with application in mind, not theoretically based lecture style methods. Recognizing that not all students learn in the same fashion, multiple ways to learning are encouraged and developed in the Tech Prep program. Students are encouraged to focus on what is required in the field, not in subjects or ways in which may never be fully utilized in the workplace or post-secondary education. Our need to teach information literacy skills and competencies in a hands-on environment and the goals of Tech Prep were a natural fit.

MEETING STUDENT NEEDS

Through our project we hoped to meet several existing needs. First, secondary level students active in the Tech Prep program had received library instruction at the College since 1995. In particular, students in the Allied Health fields learned how to research a disease, locate career information, identify future trends in a career path, and identify the importance of major contributors to the field of microbiology. Our project would enable us to teach students how to search for allied health related information using the Internet. Second, the development of the new Business Information Systems Program by secondary schools meant that students would need to learn how to use the Internet both as a communications tool and as a source of information. In our project, students and teachers at the secondary school level would converse with community college faculty and students, collaborating on projects and sharing ideas. Third, teachers and school media specialists would need to be educated on the best methods to integrate this new technology effectively into instruction. This project would offer staff development training to local area school districts. Fourth, our project would also address employers' needs of having employees learn the fourth "R"–being able to access and use information in a mostly electronic environment. Business partners involved in Tech Prep would have the opportunity to receive training on using the Internet effectively. Finally, our project responded to changing work-force needs. Educating users for the job market, one of the goals of community colleges, calls for educators at all levels to teach students new, usable skills for employment. This is reinforced by the Secretary of Labor's Commission on Achieving Necessary Skills (SCANS) Report which strongly recommends that students learn to acquire, use, organize, and evaluate information in their formal education.[5]

PROJECT OUTCOMES

We anticipated that at the end of our project the following outcomes would have been met:

- Students would be able to understand the broad framework of the information chain and process of publication.
- Students would be able to develop a research question.
- Students would be able to search for, locate, and evaluate information, regardless of format, to meet their information needs.
- Students would be assessed through a variety of measures, such as pre- and post-testing, the development of a bibliography, completion of a research project, or completion of performance tasks.

There is no question that our project was ambitious. We are committed to teaching students lifelong learning skills of information literacy–not only the skills involved with finding information but the critical thinking skills needed to conceptually create a researchable question and critical thinking skills needed to evaluate information for quality, timeliness, appropriateness, and credibility. We sought to create a project that would strengthen the bridge between secondary and higher education by teaching students to be effective in using information for problem solving.

THE PROJECT ITSELF

The proposal was submitted and received full funding for two years. Our goals were to purchase and install equipment, conduct a needs assessment, design instruction, and teach faculty and students. Once funding was received, purchasing equipment was the first priority. Working through the campus computer center, computers, printers, and software were selected and purchased. Companies with state contracts were identified. Initially, eight Pentium multimedia computers with a laser printer were purchased under the grant. Four more computers were purchased with matching college funds. Networking this equipment to the campus network and the Internet was completed.

We also needed to identify a suitable space for building the classroom. The Library lacked a large enough space to house a computer lab of 12 computers which could be expanded to 24 computers and an instructor's workstation. A two step plan was devised. Step one involved placing 12 computers and one printer into one of the larger study rooms. Although slightly claustrophobic, this room could house up to 12 computers. Working with computer center staff, equipment in Phase One was installed successfully during the 1996-97 academic year. Faculty and secondary school teachers and students involved in Tech Prep were given instruction as soon as the lab became available.

Phase Two of building the computer lab is in progress. Through relocation of public relations services, a room in the basement of the Library which once housed the photography lab and publications designer became available. This room is being remodeled with new electrical wiring, network connection, and lighting. Funding for renovations is supported by both the Tech Prep grant and administrative support. Computer equipment and networking will be completed Summer 1998. We are looking forward to moving into a larger facility and to be able to expand our seating capacity to 24 computers.

DESIGNING EFFECTIVE INSTRUCTION

A major objective of this project was not only to build a hands-on learning facility but also to develop and teach faculty and students how to search the Internet effectively for information. Instructional design took patience and planning. The first step was to conduct a needs assessment of faculty experience with computers and the Internet.

The Director of Tech Prep and Coordinator of Library Instruction created a one page needs assessment survey.[6] Faculty were asked to complete the survey prior to instruction. Results of the needs assessment showed that many faculty had computer, word processing, and spreadsheet skills but few had Internet searching skills. Faculty expressed concern that students knew more than they did about the Internet and recognized the importance of needing to be able to navigate the Internet effectively to locate information and also to integrate it effectively into instruction.

Taking into account faculty learning needs, instruction was designed. Actual instruction is two hours in length. Instruction includes mixed teaching techniques: lecture, demonstration, video, and hands-on learning. Using a variety of teaching methods addresses participants' different learning styles.[7] The overall goal of this workshop was to teach session participants to search the Internet effectively for information.

Upon completion of instruction, students and faculty have learned to:

- Create a research strategy.
- Understand the information chain and where to look for information.
- Search the Internet by Uniform Resource Locator (URL), by Search Engine, by Directory, and by Metasearch Engine.
- Evaluate the information found.
- Cite web sites in APA and MLA formats.

Instructional materials were designed and provided to workshop participants. Materials included handouts on developing a research strategy, effectively searching the Internet, quick Internet search tips, evaluating information, citing information from the World Wide Web, Internet sites to visit, and an evaluating Internet information worksheet.[8]

Instruction begins by showing *The Amazing Internet*, a 20 minute videotape which provides an easy-to-understand overview of the Internet.[9] An explanation of how information is created is given by the librarian. Workshop participants are then taken to the computer lab where hands-on instruction on how to search the Internet and how to evaluate the information found is given. Instructional materials are used for activities. Session participants are given about one-half hour at the end of class to explore topics of interest to them, ask questions, and to complete the evaluating the Internet information worksheet.

During the first year of using the electronic library instruction classroom, 60 Tech Prep teachers, students, and NCCC faculty were taught. Faculty and students came from diverse disciplines including Allied Health, Applied Communications, Applied Math, Business Information Systems, Business/Office Technology, and Engineering. Local area guidance counselors involved with the Tech Prep project also received instruction.

FUTURE PLANS

Feedback from students and faculty regarding the instruction they received in a hands-on learning environment has been very positive. Most participants commented that they were able to take the concepts and skills learned in the workshop and apply it to searching the Internet at their school and at home. One participant said that she had "received less than stellar instruction at another school on the Internet but that this was by far the most informative and easy-to-understand instruction" she received.

Also, as a result of workshop participants mentioning that they would like to share ideas and activities with other grant participants, we created a web site. Through Tech Prep grant funding, two people were hired to input Internet information and design the Web site. Response from faculty, students, and the business community has been supportive.

Having received such positive reinforcement, we are making future plans. In the coming years we hope to:

- Complete the library instruction computer classroom.
- Conduct site visits to local area secondary school media centers.
- Continue to add to our Tech Prep web site, including showcasing our "Best Practices" of effective learning activities.
- Continue to teach information literacy sessions looking at advanced search concepts and skills.
- Develop faculty, teacher, and student projects linking secondary schools and the college.

REFLECTIONS ON OUR PROJECT

In the end, we hope that our outcomes of giving students and faculty an opportunity to learn information literacy skills and concepts, to give secondary school students who might not otherwise think of college as an option an opportunity to experience higher education, and to provide teachers with information on how to integrate the Internet into curricula will have been met.

Would we do this all over again? Certainly. What was thought of as an impossibility because of budget and staffing considerations has become a reality. Strengthening relationships–between secondary schools and the college, between students and faculty–has occurred. Learning in a hands-on environment, through observation and informal feedback, appears to have resulted in retention of information literacy concepts and skills. A teaching/learning community has been created for what was thought of as non-college bound students. Students and faculty have not only learned how to search the Internet effectively for information but now have a place to return to in the web site to obtain current information on the project plus converse with one another. All of this because we decided to "think out of the box" and try a different approach to funding this project. Our best advice to readers is to look at your situation in a different light, from a different angle, and be creative in your approach to obtaining funding.

REFERENCES

1. Salony, Mary F. "The history of bibliographic instruction: changing trends from books to the electronic world." In *Library Instruction Revisited: Bibliographic Instruction Comes of Age*, edited by Lynne M. Martin, 31-51. New York: The Haworth Press, Inc., 1995.

2. Dale, Edgar. *Audio-Visual Methods in Teaching*. 3rd ed. Austin, TX: Holt, Rinehart and Winston, 1969.

3. Sternberg, Hilary. "Internet resources for grants and foundations." *College & Research Libraries News* no. 5 (1997): 314-317.

4. Falcone, Lisa and Robert Murdhenk. *Tech Prep Associate Degree Challenge*. Washington, DC: American Association of Community Colleges Publications, 1994. See also Parnell, Dale. *The Neglected Majority*. Washington, DC: Community College Press, 1985.

5. U.S. Dept. of Labor. Secretary's Commission on Achieving Necessary Skills. *What Work Requires of Schools: A SCANS Report for America 2000*. Washington, DC: GPO, June 1991, xvii.

6. You may obtain a copy of the Needs Assessment at the Niagara County Community College, Niagara County Tech Prep Consortium web site, http://www.sunyniagara.cc.ny.us/techprep/needs.html.

7. Litzinger, Mary Ellen and Bonnie Osif. "Accommodating diverse learning styles: designing instruction for electronic information sources." In *What Is Good Instruction Now? Library Instruction for the 90s*, edited by Linda Shirato, 81. Ann Arbor, MI: Pierian Press, 1993.

8. For complete details on instruction, see the NCCC Tech Prep web site at: http://www.sunyniagara.cc.ny.us/techprep/ili.html Materials available on this web site may be copied for educational purposes with permission.

9. *The Amazing Internet*. 20 min. Lancaster, PA: Classroom Connect, n.d.

Media Reference Sources
for an Academic Library

Kristine R. Brancolini

SUMMARY. On the surface many media reference questions seem simple to answer. However, the lack of reference tools often hinders the reference librarian's ability to answer even the most straightforward query. In some cases, the library simply has an inadequate collection, lacking necessary sources. In other cases, the reference tools simply do not exist. Experienced academic media librarians develop toolkits, consisting of published sources and Internet sources that allow us to provide quality reference service, despite the challenges. The appended annotated bibliography represents one librarian's media reference toolkit. Although some of the sources will vary from library to library, many of these sources are essential to effective media reference work regardless of the specific institution. *[Article copies available for a fee from The Haworth Document Delivery Service: 1-800-342-9678. E-mail address: getinfo@haworthpressinc.com]*

KEYWORDS. Reference service, media sources, media bibliography, media librarians

The following selection of media reference questions represents the types of questions media librarians answer daily. Many of them seem easy to answer but present challenges to even the most experienced librarian.

Kristine R. Brancolini is Head, Media and Reserve Services, Main Library W101A, Indiana University, Bloomington, IN 47405.

[Haworth co-indexing entry note]: "Media Reference Sources for an Academic Library." Brancolini, Kristine R. Co-published simultaneously in *The Reference Librarian* (The Haworth Information Press, an imprint of The Haworth Press, Inc.) No. 65, 1999, pp. 89-101; and: *Reference Services and Media* (ed: Martha Merrill) The Haworth Information Press, an imprint of The Haworth Press, Inc., 1999, pp. 89-101. Single or multiple copies of this article are available for a fee from The Haworth Document Delivery Service [1-800-342-9678, 9:00 a.m. - 5:00 p.m. (EST). E-mail address: getinfo@haworthpressinc. com].

- Who directed *El Norte*? Is it available on laserdisc? Does the library own it? Is the library copy subtitled or dubbed?
- Does the library have a videorecording with Martin Luther King's "I have a dream" speech? What about a compact disc with the speech? If not, will you buy it?
- Does the library have a recent video–within the past year–on the effectiveness of the Head Start Program?
- Does the library have a video showing the home video footage of the Rodney King beating? Can I buy that video or another one with the same footage? What would it cost?
- Does the library have videos of urban redevelopment projects?
- Can you show me a list of videos that teach American Sign Language? Which of the titles on the list are the best?
- Can you show me a list of films and videos featuring the dancer Doris Humphreys? Are they available for sale? Could I borrow them on interlibrary loan?
- For a class presentation, I need a video that discusses ways to prevent date rape. Does the library have one? If not, could I borrow one? Which one is the best?
- Does the library have a video of masked dance? If not, could the library buy one for me to use with my class next semester?
- Does the library have audiocassettes with T. S. Eliot reading his own poetry? Can I buy copies anywhere? How much would they cost?
- What is DVD? How does is differ from Divx? Will the library be buying either DVD or Divx video within the next year?

And here is the most important question of all: Do academic media librarians have the necessary tools to answer these questions? Unfortunately, we do not have adequate reference sources to answer all of these questions. The publications simply do not exist, on paper or electronically. As in other areas of reference work, media librarians often find other librarians to be the best sources of information. When a user brings you the plot of a movie you have never seen–no director, no performers, no date, no words from the title–human resources are your only hope of finding an answer.

For most of the questions above, the librarian begins with the local online catalog. However, inadequate cataloging often hinders the search. Even when a media resource collection has been cataloged according to standards, the records may fail to provide necessary information. For example, our copy of *Eyes on the Prize* is cataloged as a series with only a list of individual titles. Which part focuses on the Voting Rights Act? A user would have to look at the backs of boxes or the distributor's catalog to find out.

Another major problem is the lack of comprehensive finding aids. Notice that most reference questions are actually collection development or selection questions. In some cases the librarian needs evaluative tools; in other cases we need descriptive tools. Evaluative questions are often easier to answer since there are review sources for media resources. However, there is no "video in print" or "audio in print," although some of the sources listed below purport to be those sources. The most frequent reference question–and one of the most difficult to answer–is: Is [*Title of Film*] available on video? Media librarians quickly learn that OCLC WorldCat is actually the best guide to distributors of media resources. If an older theatrical film (more than about a year old) is not in OCLC, it probably has not been released on video. For home video, retail catalogs (e.g., Facets Multi-Media, 800/331-6197; and Movies Unlimited, 800/4-MOVIES) offer more reliable coverage than most of the published reference sources. For educational video, we must rely on OCLC, *Bowker's Complete Video Directory*, and *Video Source Book*. Often, the best source of information about educational video is the distributor's catalog; a current collection of catalogs is an essential reference tool.

To cope with some these gaps in the sources, academic media librarians have developed a toolkit consisting of reference books, general and specialized; review periodicals; CD-ROM databases, and Internet resources, including listservs, online newsletters, and web sites. The following selected annotated bibliography represents this toolkit.

MEDIA REFERENCE SOURCES
FOR AN ACADEMIC LIBRARY:
A SELECTED ANNOTATED BIBLIOGRAPHY

Reference Books–General

AV Market Place. New York: R.R. Bowker. (Annual).

Comprehensive directory of audio and video products, manufacturers, services, and suppliers in the United States and Canada. Over

1,200 producers or services are listed, and contact information is given for over 5,000 companies. Contains addresses and telephone numbers for the major distributors of audiovisual materials and services.

Audio Books on the Go: A Listener's Guide to Books on Cassette. Edited by Robin F. Whitten. Castine, ME: Country Roads Press, 1995.

The editor of *AudioFile* (see Review Periodicals below) has compiled reviews for recommended titles published between June 1992 and January 1995. This is a complete guide for selecting and using audiobooks with an article on evaluating audiobooks, a list of resources, advice on the care and use of audiobooks, and more. The 400 reviews are divided into broad categories, such as popular fiction, classics, history and biography. There is also a title index. This is a valuable resource for any library that collects spoken word audio.

Bowker's Complete Video Directory. New York: R.R. Bowker. Volumes 1 and 2: Entertainment. Volumes 3 and 4: Educational/Special Interest. (Annual)

Self-proclaimed "the most extensive listing of currently available Entertainment titles, as well as Education & Special Interest video for home, school, and business." All 152,000 video titles listed are in active distribution Descriptive and ordering information is presented for each title. Separate indexes are by title, genre, cast/director, awards, Spanish language, laser disc, close-captioned, manufacturers and distributors, and services and suppliers. Special section for latest releases. Each entry includes bibliographic information. Includes DVD as of the 1998 edition. Replaces *Variety's Complete Home Video Directory.* For a description of the CD-ROM version, *Variety's Complete Video Directory Plus*, see the CD-ROM section.

The Equipment Directory of Video, Computers and Audiovisual Products. Fairfax, VA: ICIA. (Annual)

A publication of ICIA (International Communications Industries Association), the trade association of the communications technologies industry. The directory provides a comprehensive list of audiovisual, computer, and video hardware, including factual information on models, price, format, weight, dimensions, power, and so on. A small reference section containing trade names and corresponding manufacturers and a glossary of technical terms. The concluding portion contains alphabetized sections on ICIA members who provide a variety of services–production, consultation, marketing, international dealers, and associates.

Film and Video Finder. Albuquerque, NM: National Information Center for Educational Media (NICEM). Latest edition 1997.

A non-evaluative source that is a bibliographic guide to commercially-produced 16mm films and videotapes. It contains approximately 123,000 entries from information culled from the Library of Congress and approximately 14,000 producers and distributors. Materials in this publication are primarily educational; there are no listings for feature-length Hollywood films or videos. This publication contains the same information as found on the CD-ROM product *A-V Online*; the database is also available on a subscription basis as *NICEM Net* (*http://www.nicem.com/*), which is updated bi-weekly.

Multimedia and Videodisc Compendium. St. Paul: MN: Emerging Technology Consultants. Annual.

This annual publication is updated quarterly. Organized by four major subjects, "Business and Industry," "Education," "Health," and "Technology," broken down into further subcategories, this volume also has a title index. The entries are color coded to differentiate CD-ROMs from laserdiscs. These are all educational products rather than consumer-oriented. Annotated entries include prices and complete ordering information.

Pratt, Douglas. *The Laser Video Disc Compendium, 1995 Edition.* New York: Baseline, 1995.

The editor and publisher of *The Laser Video Disc Newsletter* compiles his laserdisc reviews from time to time. The 1995 edition contains reviews for domestic and imported laserdiscs from the beginning of the 1980s through September 1994. In addition to the reviews, this volume includes a list with every laserdisc released in the United States during this time period. Pratt's introductory essay places the reviews in context. Appendix B, "One Hundred Great Laser Discs," is not to be missed.

Spencer, James R. *Spencer's Complete Guide to Special Interest Videos.* Scottsdale, AZ: James-Robert Publishers. (Biennial). Latest edition 1998. Alternate title *Complete Guide to Special Interest Videos.*

Spencer has organized over 10,000 entries according to 41 subject categories, such as Automotive, Business, Computers, Cooking, Dance, and so on, with a title index at the back of the book. All videos are in print. Each entry includes complete ordering information, a short annotation, a review citation if available, IBSN, an indication of public performance rights, price, and more. Although many of the titles listed in Spencer's publication are more suitable for public libraries than academic libraries, I have found this book to be extremely useful for answering reference questions. Also available on CD-ROM.

Video Source Book. Detroit: Gale Research. 2 volumes. (Annual)

According to *Reference Books Bulletin, Video Source Book* is the single "most comprehensive listing of available video programs." It provides a complete and relatively up-to-date reference to video-in-print, attempting to list every type of program available in all formats, including Beta, VHS, Laserdisc, DVD (as of 1998) 8 mm video cartridge, and 3/4″ U-matic. Lists and describes more than 120,000 listings representing 160,000 programs currently available on video in all areas of entertainment, educational and cultural interest, business, how-to, movies, sports, fine arts, music, religion, and documentaries. Video program sources index provides corporation's name, address, and telephone number. Acquisition availability is also included–rental, loan, purchase, duplication, subscription, trade-in, free duplication, duplication license, and off-air recording.

Words on Cassette. New Providence, N.J.: R.R. Bowker. 2 volumes. (Annual)

A comprehensive look at the contemporary marketplace of spoken word audiocassettes. This directory of 57,000 titles from over 2,000 producers reflects the merging of Meckler's *Words on Tape* with Bowker's *On Cassette.* Indexes are arranged by title, author, reader/performer, subject, and producer/distributor. Subjects include materials for both children and adults with a broad range of topics–novels, self-help, business, poetry, history, biography, literary and political reviews. Lists the Best Audiobooks and Audie Award winners from 1994 to the present. This publication is as close to a "spoken word audio in print" as you will find.

Reference Books-Specialized

Dance on Camera: A Guide to Dance Films and Videos. Edited by Louise Spain. Lanham, MD: The Scarecrow Press; New York: Neal-Schuman Publishers, 1998.

Louise Spain, an academic media librarian, has compiled a resource for members of the dance profession, educators, librarians, curators, programmers, producers, directors, and those interested in dance on film and video. This revised and updated version of *Dance Film and Video Guide* (1991) includes over 1,400 entries; 400 new titles and 100 new entries for musical dance feature films. To be listed, films and videotapes had to be in current distribution in the United States. In addition to the alphabetical listing by title, this volume includes introductory essays and numerous indexes.

Lems-Dworkin, Carol. *Videos of African and African-Related Performance: An Annotated Bibliography.* Evanston, IL: Carol Lems-Dworkin Publishers, 1996.

Lems-Dworkin's annotated guide to in-print African performance videos represents an important genre of media reference sources. I have used this book to locate extremely specialized videos that I could not have located using general reference sources. The primary purpose of this book is to "help people locate videos showing aspects of African or African-related performance." The 1,396 videos span the entire continent of Africa, its islands, the Americas, and several European countries. The book includes a User's Guide, a Names Index, a Subject Index, and a Distributors Index.

Stevens, Gregory I. *Videos for Understanding Diversity: A Core Selection and Evaluative Guide.* Chicago: American Library Association, 1993.

Thirty scholars from New York state selected the 126 videos they believed were "most clearly associated with facets of multicultural education, as well as those best illustrating the range of topics within the subject areas." Each signed entry includes purchase and rental information, including prices, a description of content, suggestions for classroom use, and critical comments. There is a Title-Theme Index and a Categorical Index. Although it is becoming somewhat dated, many of the titles includes in this guide are classics.

Index to Reviews

Media Review Digest. Ann Arbor, MI: Pierian Press. (Annual).

The only complete guide to reviews of non-print media. An index and digest of reviews, evaluations, and descriptions appearing in periodicals and reviewing sources. The listings are divided under the following headings (in 1997; these categories change with format changes): Film and Video, Audio, CD-ROM, and Miscellaneous Media. *MRD* contains approximately 42,000 citations per volume, indexing 150 periodicals and services. The indexes include General Subject Indicators, Subject Index, Reviewers' Index, Geographical Index, Producer/Distributor Directory, and Periodicals/Services Index. The most current volume contains reviews for the previous year's non-print media materials.

Review Periodicals

AudioFile: The Monthly Newletter of Audio Reviews. Portland, ME. (Monthly)

This unique resource reviews spoken word audiocassettes. Each issue includes a feature article and short reviews, divided into various categories, depending upon the issue content. Evaluative criteria include narrative voice and style, vocal characterizations, appropriateness for audio format, and enhancement of the text. "Truly exceptional presentations" received a little headphones symbol. Reviews are initialed and the list of reviewers includes librarians, educators, authors, and audiophiles. If your library buys spoken word audio, you should subscribe to this reasonably-priced publication.

Video Librarian. Bremerton, WA: Randy Pitman. (Monthly)

Primarily focused on the needs of public librarians, Randy Pitman's *Video Librarian* includes short articles and lengthy starred reviews in each issue. Reviews are divided into the following categories: children's, documentaries, how-to, library science, miscellaneous, and "In brief." Pitman is a leading proponent of video services in public libraries. Until 1992 he also published a column on "video movies," independent features, in *Library Journal.* He has recently begun covering independent theatrical releases again in *Video Librarian.*

With the volume 11, number 1, January-February 1996 issue, *Video Librarian* has a slicker, more professional look. Pitman has expanded his scope from newsletter to magazine. He has also added reviewers; he is no longer the sole reviewer. *Video Librarian* is also on the Web *(http://www.videolibrarian.com/)* with selected reviews, news briefs, and more.

CD-ROM Databases

A-V Online. Albuquerque, NM: National Information Center for Educational Media (NICEM). (Updated quarterly)

A database of distribution sources for educational media currently available. Formats included are 16mm film, video, filmstrips, audiotape, slide sets, phonodiscs, transparency sets, and 8mm film. Users can limit the search by age of intended audience, media format, dates, length of presentation, producer, color, black and white, and subject. Contains the same material listed in *Film and Video Finder*, plus all of the other NICEM databases, but updated much more frequently.

Variety's Video Directory Plus. New York: Bowker. (Updated semi-annually)

Essentially, the CD-ROM version of *Bowker's Complete Video Directory*, plus film reviews from *Variety.* However, there are over 165,000 citations in the database and only 5,500 reviews. The database is searchable in numerous ways including title, keyword in title, performer/director, keyword, subject/genre, year produced, year released on video, and more. Useful as a reference/verification tool, the CD-ROM product can also be used to produce order forms.

Internet Resources

Listservs

When all else fails, consult an expert! The two video lists are sponsored by the Video Round Table of American Library Association (*http://www.lib.virginia.edu/dmmc/VRT/*). Gary Handman manages both lists, but they are unmoderated.

Audiobooks

Audiobooks is sponsored by the Audio Publishers Association, a not-for-profit trade association dedicated to promoting awareness of Spoken Word Audio (Audiobooks). Many subscribers post lengthy reviews, and publishers post information about new releases. This list tends to be a little chatty–kind of like a big audiobooks fan club–but many of the major publishers, readers, and audiobook sellers subscribe, so it's a good source of information. To subscribe, send the usual subscription message [subscribe "yourname" audiobooks], with a blank subject line, to listserv@hrsys.hslc.org.

Videolib

Videolib is a discussion group for video librarians, producers/distributors, and anyone interested in issues related to media librarianship. Most of the messages are queries about the availability of a particular title: Does anyone know a distributor? What's the price? Does anyone know a rental source? There are also general acquisitions questions: What's a good source for out-of-print video? Could anyone recommend some videos on aboriginal art of Australia? Subscribers also discuss copyright and other issues. To subscribe, send the usual subscription message to listserv@library.berkeley.edu.

Videonews

Videonews provides distributors with an opportunity to advertise new releases or special promotions. This listserv grew out of a need for distributors to share information with librarians, but it wasn't seen as appropriate for Videolib. Librarians who want this type of information can receive it by subscribing to Videonews; commercial activity can be avoided on Videolib by offering an alternative listserv. Send the usual subscription message to listserv@library.berkeley.edu

Online Newletters

Laser Scans: The Laserdisc and DVD Newsletter, a monthly newsletter distributed online, is edited and published by Chris McGowan. Email subscriptions are free. To subscribe, email Chris McGowan at LaserScans@aol.com. Laser Scans is available at the following Web sites:

- CyberTheater: The Internet Journal of Home Theater *(http://www. cybertheater.com/laserscans_idx.html)*
- Cinema.lu: Info and New About Movies for Luxembourg *(http://www.cinema.lu/laserscans/)*
- Home Theater Connection *(http://www.h-t-c.com/LaserScans.html)*

PBS Previews. Weekly newsletter of PBS Online, the website of the Public Broadcasting Service. Highlights additions to the website. To subscribe, send an email message to www@pbs.org. In the body of the message type: sub web-update. Subscription is free. You can also obtain subscription information by going to PBS Online *(http://pbs.org)*.

Web Sites

CineMedia
http://www.afionline.org/CINEMEDIA/CineMedia.home.html

With links to 18,000 sites, *CineMedia* may well be "the Internet's largest film and media directory," as it claims on its banner. Sponsored by the American Film Institute, *CineMedia* is not as academic as *ScreenSite*, but it does includes links to thousands of valuable reference sites. Users can browse one of 16 categories or search for specific topics.

Media Resources Center. Moffitt Library, University of California Berkeley
http://www.lib.berkeley.edu/MRC/

Gary Handman, Head, Media Resources Center, has created the model Web site for academic library media centers at University of

California Berkeley. Until we are able to create equally wonderful Web sites at our institutions, we can link to his and benefit from his work. Actually, like Corinne Smith's Web publication below, there would be no point in duplicating the hard work that went into creating many of these Web pages. The following two pages exemplify types of information Handman has compiled:

- "Film & Video Distributors & Producers"
  http://www.lib.berkeley.edu/MRC/Distributors.html
- "Media Reference Sources & Information"
  http://www.lib.berkeley.edu/MRC/FilmRefMenu.html

The first is a list that Handman created with addresses, phone numbers, email addresses, and Web sites for distributors and producers of educational and educational films and videos. The second is a compilation of links to other media reference sources.

Public Affairs Video Archive. Purdue University, West Lafayette, Indiana
http://www.pava.purdue.edu

The Public Affairs Video Archives was established at Purdue University to record, index, and archive all C-SPAN programming. A searchable database indexes over 70,000 hours of C-SPAN programming, every program aired since 1987. The Archives records both C-SPAN networks seven days a week, 24-hours a day. Programs are indexed by subject, speaker names, titles, affiliations, sponsors, committees, categories, formats, policy groups, keywords, and location. Individuals and libraries can purchase duplicate copies of most C-SPAN programs that have aired since 1987.

ScreenSite. http://www.tcf.ua.edu/screensite/welcome.htm

Sponsored by The University of Alabama, the College of Communication, and the Department of Telecommunication and Film, *"Screen-Site"* emerged from a desire to provide access to film and television resources through the World Wide Web. Its primary purpose is to facilitate the study of film/TV. As opposed to some Web sites that take more of a fan's approach to the media, ScreenSite stresses the teaching and research of film and television and is designed for educators and students" (Introduction). Founded in 1994, *ScreenSite* is an extremely well-organized and well-maintained Web site.

Smith, Corinne. *"I Saw It on TV": A Guide to Broadcast and Cable Programming Sources.* Last updated August 21, 1997
http://www.library.nwu.edu/media/resources/tvguide.html

Corinne Smith, Librarian, Elgin High School, Elgin, Illinois, compiled the first edition of this guide in 1994. It includes addresses, phone, numbers, email addresses, and URLs for broadcast and cable networks in the United States and Canada, commercial sources, transcripts, production companies, and much more. This is an essential source for media librarians.

Vanderbilt Television News Archive. http://tvnews.vanderbilt.edu

Since August 5, 1968, the Vanderbilt Television News Archive has systematically recorded, abstracted, and indexed national television newscasts. This Web site is the guide to the Vanderbilt University collection of network television news programs. The collection represents a unique reference source as borrowers throughout the world may make videotape loan requests for reference, study, classroom instruction, and research.

Providing a State-Wide Digital Library: A Voyage of Discovery

Theresa Plummer
Ed McNeeley

SUMMARY. The State Library of Delaware has brought *DelAWARE*: The Digital Library of the First State into being in regular, steady increments. Providing a digital library for a state library network, no matter how small, is always a project both blessed with support systems and fraught with unforeseen obstacles. You just never know what will happen next or who will show up to save the day.

By steadfastly working and collaborating with all partners (librarians, vendors, state agencies), *DelAWARE*: The Digital Library of the First State is being brought into existence, a product at a time. By addressing the needs and difficulties of its users, the digital library grows into something uniquely useful for the state and its citizens. *[Article copies available for a fee from The Haworth Document Delivery Service: 1-800-342-9678. E-mail address: getinfo@haworthpressinc.com]*

KEYWORDS. Digital library, public libraries, electronic library, *Del*AWARE

Delaware is a small state. It goes about its business quietly, incorporating companies, handling credit card debt, developing chemical products. "Below the canal," in southern Delaware, they raise chick-

Theresa Plummer and Ed McNeeley are Administrative Librarians/Digital Resources, Delaware Division of Libraries/The State Library, 43 S. DuPont Highway, Dover, DE 19901.

[Haworth co-indexing entry note]: "Providing a State-Wide Digital Library: A Voyage of Discovery." Plummer, Theresa, and Ed McNeeley. Co-published simultaneously in *The Reference Librarian* (The Haworth Information Press, an imprint of The Haworth Press, Inc.) No. 65, 1999, pp. 103-110; and: *Reference Services and Media* (ed: Martha Merrill) The Haworth Information Press, an imprint of The Haworth Press, Inc., 1999, pp. 103-110. Single or multiple copies of this article are available for a fee from The Haworth Document Delivery Service [1-800-342-9678, 9:00 a.m. - 5:00 p.m. (EST). E-mail address: getinfo@haworthpressinc. com].

ens and vegetables and invite people to their beaches in summer. Delaware is a calm oasis in the midst of manic activity in other middle Atlantic states. But even Delaware can go digital. And it was one of the first.

In the early '90s, Delaware readied itself for the White House Conference on Library and Information Services with its own state-wide conference. Automation held top priority. At the time, Wilmington Institute was the only public library automated.

The General Assembly supported the endeavor with a task force of its own concluding that "automation and linking of Delaware libraries is critical for the provision of information which support the educational and life-long learning needs of Delawareans."[1]

An agreement signed in January 1994 by the Department of State (which includes the State Library as one if its divisions) and Delaware Technical & Community College (DTCC) allowing the library to link into DTTC's Internet backbone created the *Del*AWARE Library Information Network, linking all of Delaware's public libraries to the Internet and setting the stage for future resource sharing.

While libraries were gearing up for automation, the State House of Representatives passed a resolution forming a committee to develop a plan for placing computers and telecommunications in the public schools. The committee issued a report in early 1995 including a recommendation that "Delaware should recognize, designate and invest in the State Library as the electronic library for the State of Delaware available via the Internet to the public libraries, schools, colleges and general public via the networks being put in place."[2]

With political and community support, we were off and running. By November, 1995 the State Library sent a document to librarians and legislators outlining a Pilot Project to accomplish three goals:

- to provide a network infrastructure adequate for Internet access and to support the delivery of electronic information resources and services to public libraries and their customers.
- to deliver full text periodicals online to all public libraries via the network and
- to set up a technology education center at the State Library for librarians.[3]

By June of 1997 we had achieved all the objectives of the project. We had installed a Sun minicomputer and a T1 line. Starting in January, 1996, public libraries and their dial-in users could access two full text databases. Training had begun.

Library systems provided access to the digital library as they were automated. The Wilmington Institute Library and the public libraries in Kent County were first, followed by public libraries in New Castle County and DTCC, and finally, the public libraries in Sussex County.

In the meantime, we had been moving ahead to design a name and a face for our electronic library. A statewide contest and a trademark name search yielded *Del*AWARE™ as the winner. The logo and name graced our first graphical homepage, designed in time for our *Del*-AWARE™ premier in October, 1996.

But, we had a problem. The system providing our full text databases had slowed down to a crawl. It was practically unusable. A check with other customers of this provider indicated that they were having similar difficulties. Days before the premier we scrambled to get a frame relay connection installed so we could show off our wonderful full text products. We did it.

The Governor, state senators and representatives were duly impressed with our Pilot Project. By means of our own authentication program, we were able to allow access to all Delawareans. Now anyone with a Delaware public library card could enter his barcode number and PIN at the *Del*AWARE™ web site (http://www.lib.de.us) and have access to over 1,600 full text periodicals.

The web site also made the state government telephone directory available to the public for the first time. At the time, this publication functioned as more of an in-house directory, used primarily by state agency staff and institutions that interacted with the state bureaucracy on a frequent basis. Considered by the State Library to be a fundamental information service to Delaware's citizens, the hard copy of the state's phone directory was not widely distributed. Now, anyone could find this information.

In addition, *Del*AWARE™ users could access state, federal and local government web pages. They could also read several state government publications, including the *Delaware Statistical Overview*, *The Corporate Edge* newsletter from the Division of Corporations and the *Governor's Recommended Budget*. A subject guide, DelaWeb, connected users to web sites. Customers could also access all public libraries in the state (as they were automated and online).

But difficulties lay ahead. In December, the provider for our fulltext databases confessed that the larger of the two files was broken and they would try to fix it. The fix dragged on for months. There was also a problem with the printer using far more paper than was necessary to print each article. Finally, the provider disclosed that they would never be able to fix the printing difficulties. A promised web-based version of their product was not becoming a reality. We still had six months to go. . . .

As the contracts drew to a close, it was obvious we couldn't renew our contract with the full text database service provider and we had to look elsewhere. By this time, however, vendors had decided to host their own products. We took a look at the three top content providers for full text periodicals and another service provider.

Now our options shifted. We would be delivering the products from a web site but this presented another difficulty. The previous provider had presented public libraries with an interface that looked exactly like the one on their OPACs. Public libraries and their customers grew comfortable with this interface. With the new products, however, they would be viewing the web resources with a Lynx text-based browser.

As we tested and evaluated the new provider and vendor/hosts, we kept several things in mind:

- All the interfaces looked fine when viewed with a graphical browser; however, we also needed to judge the interface on the basis of its usability with the Lynx browser.
- Patrons had gotten used to having both general interest and business periodicals. We needed to fulfill that expectation or exceed it.
- Once frame relay had been installed, users had the expectation of swift, consistent access. Would access over the Internet be as satisfying?
- We wanted a vendor whose technical service department would be sensitive to our difficulties and would work in a timely fashion to resolve problems.

We compared databases according to quantity, currency, and breadth and depth of content. However, the constraint of having to use the Lynx browser (several public library systems had only dumb terminals) became the overriding criterion. One vendor stood out among the others in the usability of its product with the Lynx browser. Luckily, it also turned out to have the largest collection of full text periodicals, and we were also able to access a number of subsets of its database. Finally, we were able to use this same interface to access ERIC and MEDLINE. Additionally, their technical department worked with ours to include our authentication page. There was something for everyone.

But whitewater again lay ahead. Although the Lynx browser had been in place for Internet use in public libraries for more than two years, few librarians had used it. It was clunky; there weren't many web links; they were fearful of technology; there were so few workers in their libraries, they didn't have time to use it; they had no access to a work station. When the new full text database service came online, it was not as familiar and simple to use as the older interface. They were not pleased.

The former service had looked and acted just like their OPACs. With Lynx they had to arrow up, arrow down, hit enter to open various menus, arrow down to choose, hit enter, arrow up to search, hit enter and on, and on, and on.

Those who were comfortable with Lynx didn't mind the change, and many library customers diligently worked away to get their articles. But for some, it was just frustrating. "The view wasn't worth the climb," was the way one patron put it.

Patrons who dialed into the libraries were met with the same scenario. Intrepid searchers printed off their magazine articles. Others called the library and asked for help.

Meanwhile, students at DTCC and those who came to the web site from their own Internet Service Providers searched happily. They had graphical browsers. It was clear that if *Del*AWARE: The Digital Library of the First State was going to be an effective tool for librarians and their customers, they had to have graphical browsers to use it.

Public librarians were also clamoring for hands-on training. They didn't have time or enough staff work stations to practice on their own. Unfortunately, a summer flood in 1996 had caused structural damage to the State Library. Construction of the technology education center had been set back a year. When the new training center opened in Fall of 1997, librarians were thrilled with the state of the art facility.

Librarians filled every seat of every training session we offered–and clamored for more. They wanted to be able to use full text databases, government information resources and DelaWeb web links. They wanted to be demystified by all the technology.

But they still complained about not having graphical browsers in their libraries. And, in order to accomplish that, a number of issues had to be faced:

- Legacy hardware. Some systems still had terminals which would not support graphical access. Libraries had to replace these with personal computers.
- Security issues abounded, including locking down workstations and browsers.
- Telecommunications concerns. The 56kbs lines in place were not going to be sufficient to handle the load of graphics libraries would be accessing. Increased monthly costs would also have to be considered.
- Internet use policies. Libraries and their boards would have to develop policies for the use of Internet within their libraries and determine how they would enforce them.
- Then there was the privacy issue and the filtering issue.

And all of this needed addressing, for the most part, by librarians whose libraries had been automated for the first time with host-terminal architecture. They also had to face the fact that in a couple of years they would have to upgrade to an entirely different architecture. It was daunting.

And still we kept at it. In the spring of 1997 we formed a Resource Development Team to create a Collection Development Policy for DelaWeb, our online subject guide, and to test and evaluate licensed databases for possible inclusion in *Del*AWARE ™. This team was composed of librarians from school, public and special libraries and one representative from the Division of the Arts.

With a policy in place (http://www.lib.de.us/about/cdpolicy.htm), we created an evaluation form for the selection of Web sites to include in DelaWeb. Each member of the team was responsible for the development of a "subject" in DelaWeb.

We also recruited Site Searchers from among librarians and interested individuals throughout the state. We developed training to teach searchers and team members how to evaluate sites in light of the criteria established in the Collection Development Policy. We taught them how to use review resources on the web and review resources in publications. They learned how to find listservs and newsgroups for their subjects.

Finally, since everyone was dispersed throughout the state, we set up a listserv for the Resource Development Team and a listserv for Site Searchers, which included everybody. We hoped everyone would communicate using the lists, but it was not to be. People were still not as comfortable as we hoped with technology and preferred face to face, interactive meetings.

As we developed content for DelaWeb, we also proceeded with government information. Building upon the success of the online state phone directory, we spent 1997 working with a number of state agencies to produce other demonstration projects and to improve the quality of state agency web services.

A commercial search engine was licensed early in 1998. *Del-AWARE*™ now supported the only comprehensive search of all state government web space. We also provided specialized searches of the Delaware Register and the escheat database at the Division of Revenue.

Although these efforts demonstrated *Del*AWARE's Internet expertise and provided several valuable services to the public, they actually only brought us to the real work–designing and implementing a true library of digital government information.

One of the basic challenges in building this library is the monopolistic position of the state agency as the creator/vendor of key material. In the absence of an executive mandate, which some states attempted, the individual agency decides whether to publish electronically. This decision was frequently made by staff who were low on the policy-making ladder. Decisions were often based more on personal interest in the technology than the agency's assessment of the value of the material.

If an agency decided not to publish key materials in electronic form, then there was no easy alternative source. The librarian could not turn to another content supplier and ask "what serials are in your database that relate to. . . . ?"

One option for the digital library is to establish document scanning as a primary method for electronic collection development. The equipment is expensive, the process is labor intensive and the end product (a tiff image) has less utility than the file formats available if the agency had initially published the document electronically (pdf).

Even if agencies publish the desired materials, the quality of the documents varies considerably, and the library is still challenged to develop the collection. Careless or inadvertent creation of metadata interferes with a routine discovery process, and the digital librarian needs to decide when to create a stand-alone and parallel system and when to work with the agency to create better document-based metadata.

We released Version 3 of *Del*AWARE™ in March, 1998. It included an updated home page with more user-friendly buttons to link searchers immediately to resources. It included a reorganized DelaWeb, set up according to categories in the Collection Development Policy. It contained many more web sites.

Version 3 also contained more government information including the Delaware *Register of Regulations*, access to State Legislative bills and expanded local government sites. The highlight of Version 3, however, was inclusion of the search engine to search our entire web site. Users of *Del*AWARE™ could now search all collections or limit their search to government information or DelaWeb.

The digital libraries that we build for our states will be individually crafted, finely honed products that emerge as a result of the collaboration of many individuals working to bring necessary information to those who need it. As we develop these libraries, it will become clearer what is wanted, what is needed, what is used. We will all become more sophisticated consumers of information and so these libraries will continually reinvent themselves.

REFERENCES

1. Legislative Taskforce on Library Automation, *Report of the Legislative Task Force on Library Automation to the 137th General Assembly*, State of Delaware, April 1, 1993.

2. Delaware Education Technology Committee, *Educational Technology: A Report to the Governor, Legislature and Citizens of Delaware*, February, 1995.

3. Delaware Division of Libraries/The State Library of Delaware, *A Proposal by the Delaware Division of Libraries to Implement a Pilot Project for the Electronic Library of Delaware, January 1996 to June 1997*, November 1995.

Survey of the Confidence Levels of Public Service Librarians in Using Electronic Reference Sources

Alison Hopkins
Jacquelyn Sapiie

SUMMARY. The Internet Self-Managed Work Team of the Queens Borough Public Library surveyed a stratified random sample of public service librarians to determine their confidence levels of using electronic resources to answer reference questions. Two test groups were used to fine-tune the survey instrument, and a control group of non-public service librarians was used for comparison purposes. Questions were categorized into nine types, including Internet, Catalog, Telnet and Test. The results demonstrated high confidence levels in using the Library's Catalog and lower results in using the Internet. The lowest confidence levels were for questions dealing with personal computers and handling customer complaints about the Internet. Branch size, position, or rank of the respondent did not affect confidence levels in any predictable fashion. *[Article copies available for a fee from The Haworth Document Delivery Service: 1-800-342-9678. E-mail address: getinfo@haworthpressinc. com]*

KEYWORDS. Reference questions, electronic resources, public service librarians

Alison Hopkins is affiliated with the Extension Services Department and Jacquelyn Sapiie is Reference Librarian, Information Services, both at the Queens Borough Public Library, 89-11 Merrick Boulevard, Jamaica, NY 11432.

[Haworth co-indexing entry note]: "Survey of the Confidence Levels of Public Service Librarians in Using Electronic Reference Sources." Hopkins, Alison, and Jacquelyn Sapiie. Co-published simultaneously in *The Reference Librarian* (The Haworth Information Press, an imprint of The Haworth Press, Inc.) No. 65, 1999, pp. 111-123; and: *Reference Services and Media* (ed: Martha Merrill) The Haworth Information Press, an imprint of The Haworth Press, Inc., 1999, pp. 111-123. Single or multiple copies of this article are available for a fee from The Haworth Document Delivery Service [1-800-342-9678, 9:00 a.m. - 5:00 p.m. (EST). E-mail address: getinfo@haworthpressinc.com].

BACKGROUND AND KEY TERMS

Queens Borough Public Library (QBPL) was committed to offering the Internet as well as other electronic resources to aid customers. As there were different perceptions concerning the ability of librarians to use these resources, it was important to find an objective way to measure this. In February 1996, the Internet Self-Managed Work Team (Iteam) determined to discover how confident staff librarians were in using electronic resources to answer reference questions.

The Iteam is a group of Queens Borough Public Library professional staff members dedicated to the integration of the Internet into library services at all levels. The following team members were involved with the survey project at one time or another: Jane Jacobs, Mary Little, Robyn Lupa, Natalie Power, Gordon Riley, Robert Sage and Jessica Wolfe.

At this time, only the Central Library provided public Internet access as well as an OPAC. Internet access was provided via Lynx, a text-only interface. Most branch librarians could access the Internet at reference terminals only; however, QBPL was planning Netscape access at all branches and at Central for customers and for staff.

The Queens Borough Public Library (QBPL) is located in the borough of Queens in New York City. It consists of 62 branches plus the Central Library (CEL) and employs 1,000 people, 350 of which are classified as librarians. Each branch and division within the Central Library is called an *agency*. Branches are divided into three sizes: *large*, *medium* and *small*, based on circulation, size, and staffing levels. There are 10 large branches, 34 medium branches and 28 small branches.

A *librarian*, for the purposes of this study, is defined as an individual who holds a Master's degree in library science, or who is in the Trainee program and enrolled in a Master's program. Each librarian has a *rank* as well as a *position*. Position refers to their job title and, in this study, can be one of the following five:

> *Children's Librarian* (J): A Children's Librarian is responsible for the collection, reference, programs and services for children at an agency.
> *Young Adult Librarian* (YA): A Young Adult Librarian is responsible for the collection, reference, programs and services for young adults at an agency.

General Assistant (GA): A General Assistant is responsible for the collection, reference, programs and services for adults at an agency.

Assistant Branch Library Manager/Assistant Division Head (ABLM/ADD): An Assistant Branch Library Manager is responsible for supervision of librarians and the day-to-day branch operations. An Assistant Division Head performs similar duties at CEL.

Branch Library Manager (BLM): A Branch Library Manager is responsible for all aspects of branch operations.

These categories are not mutually exclusive as a Children's Librarian may also be an Assistant Branch Library Manager.

Rank is the classification of the librarian within the system and in this study can be one of the following five.

Library Trainee (Trainee): A trainee is an individual who is hired by the Library in the expectation that the person will complete a Master's in Library Science. They are full time employees enrolled in a Master's program.

General Assistant (GA): General Assistant is the rank given to new public service librarians.

Senior Librarian (Senior): After a period of service at the Library, librarians attain the rank of Senior Librarian. To hold the position of ABLM, a librarian must be of this rank.

Supervising Librarian (Super): A Supervising Librarian holds the position of BLM at a medium branch, ABLM at a large branch, or ADD at CEL.

Principal Librarian (Princ): A Principal Librarian holds the position of BLM at a large branch.

The control group included librarians in other than public service positions. They included:

Catalog Division (CAT): Catalogers perform professional and technical activities such as cataloging.

Programs and Services Department (PSD): Members of this department organize and design special programs and services for the agencies of the library.

In this study, the *Library Catalog* is defined as the QBPL Online Catalog. It includes other databases accessible through the catalog such as the magazine databases.

HYPOTHESES

A. Librarians at the QBPL are more confident answering reference questions using the Library Catalog than the Internet.
B. Public service librarians are more confident answering reference questions using electronic resources than non-public service librarians (control group).
C. Branch size is a determining variable for the confidence levels of librarians in answering reference questions using electronic resources.
D. Position is a determining variable for the confidence levels of librarians in answering reference questions using electronic resources.
E. Rank is a determining variable for the confidence levels of librarians in answering reference questions using electronic resources.
F. Test questions will have a lower confidence levels than all other question types.

METHODOLOGY

The Electronic Resources survey was developed to measure the confidence of QBPL public service librarians in answering specific reference questions using electronic resources. Respondents were asked to check off their rank and position as well as their level of confidence in answering 31 questions using electronic resources. The five levels of confidence ranged from "I would not know how to solve this problem" to "I am certain I could solve this problem." Of the 31 questions, three could be answered using the Library Catalog, one using the Library's gopher, one using the Community Services database, one was a policy question, seven were difficult to impossible to do using electronic resources while the remaining eighteen could be answered using the Internet.

Two test groups, one including Internet competent individuals and the other Internet novices, were selected to complete the survey. The reactions of the test groups resulted in changes in directions as well as the wording of specific questions.

A control group of sixteen librarians, eight members of the Cataloging Department and eight members of the Programs and Services Department, was selected to complete the survey.

A random sample of librarians was selected from the system to take this survey. In order to ensure that librarians from all parts of the system were included, libraries were divided into four categories: small, medium, large and CEL. These categories already exist as part of the Library's organizational structure as referred to previously. The number of librarians selected from each category was determined by equating the ratio of (librarians at each size of branch)/(librarians in system) to (librarians at each size of branch surveyed)/(librarians surveyed). Then, playing cards were used for a random drawing in each category. Three alternates were included in each category to account for inaccuracies in the rosters from which subjects were selected. A total of 59 participants were selected, 51 of whom completed the survey.

The survey and instructions were sent through inter-office mail to the selected participants. Its completion was mandatory. They were instructed to return the survey in an envelope indicating their agency. The envelope was used to determine which participants had completed the survey. Once this information was recorded, the branch size was written on the survey and separated from the envelope so that no individual survey could be linked to a particular respondent. E-mail from supervisors as well as follow-up phone calls were used to encourage individuals to complete the surveys.

LIMITATIONS OF THE STUDY

The unpredictability of the respondents' methods is the greatest limiting factor of the survey instrument. When first analyzing the data, one assumes that all respondents read the instructions and answered in good faith, but this is not necessarily so. Also, respondents may not answer honestly, wishing to seem more knowledgeable. Test questions were used in an attempt to measure if respondents were answering based on experience. Test questions were very difficult to answer, and if respondents were answering based on experience, they would indicate lower confidence levels than other questions.

While respondents were instructed to allow adequate time to answer the survey, there is no way to determine if this was done. Some may have completed the survey quickly, while others may have taken much more time.

Another potential problem is that some reference questions can be answered without using electronic resources. The high confidence level for question 26 concerning booksales at agencies, for example, is probably more related to the fact that each branch has a printed list of monthly booksales than indicating that the respondents knew the list was located on the Library's gopher.

Finally, it is important to remember that the survey measured confidence levels. The survey measured what respondents believe they could do rather than what they could actually do. In some ways, this study is examining the individual's perception of what information is available using electronic resources, and how easy it is to obtain.

DATA ANALYSIS

Data were entered on a spreadsheet and sorted. The questions were divided into nine types according to what skills would be needed in order to answer the reference questions. The types were:

> *Catalog:* questions 1, 21, and 25 are answerable using the Library's Catalog
> *ComS:* question 4 could be answered using the Community Services Database
> *E-mail:* question 2 could be answered using E-mail skills
> *FTP:* question 6 could be answered using FTP (file transfer protocol) skills
> *Internet:* questions 3, 10, 12, 13, 14, 15, 18, 19, 22, 23, 24, 27, 28, and 31 are answerable using Internet skills excluding FTP and telnet
> *PC:* question 11 could be answered using Personal Computing knowledge
> *Policy:* question 29 is related to the policy of the Library
> *Qgopher:* question 26 could be answered using the Queens Library gopher

Telnet: question 5 could be answered using telnet skills
Test: questions 7, 8, 9, 16, 17, 20, and 30 ranged from difficult to impossible to answer

Each possible confidence level was given a number as follows:

5 I am certain I could answer this question
4 I am confident I could answer this question
3 I might be able to answer this question
2 I doubt that I could solve this problem
1 I would not know how to solve this problem

Average confidence levels by question type were then calculated and compared by branch size, position and rank of the respondents. In all three cases, there is no measurable difference in average confidence level in answering reference questions. In all three instances, Catalog questions had a higher confidence level than Internet questions. E-mail, Qgopher, and the ComS questions demonstrated a higher level than both Catalog or Internet questions (Figures 1-2).

Then the average confidence levels of the control group were compared to the average confidence levels of Senior Librarians (Figure 3). The Control Group consisted of senior librarians in non-public service positions and thus can be compared to senior librarians in public service positions. The levels were very similar for most question types, the difference between each being no larger than 1 confidence level. The control group demonstrated higher average confi-

FIGURE 1. Question Types by Rank of Librarian

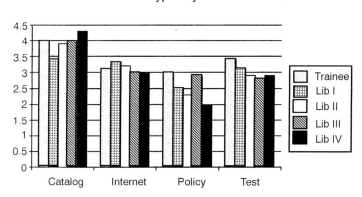

FIGURE 2. Question Types by Library Size

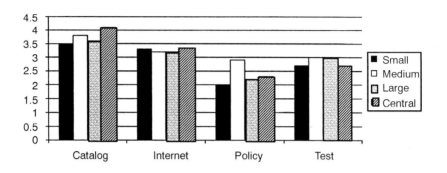

FIGURE 3. Public Service Librarians Compared to Non-Public Service Librarians

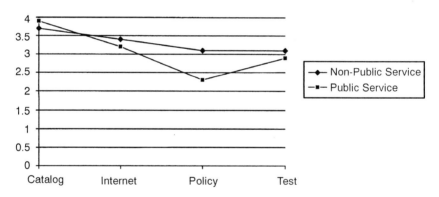

dence levels for most question types, especially E-mail, Policy and PC. Lower average confidence levels appear only for Qgopher and Catalog question types. For ease of analysis, the focus was on only four question types; Catalog, Internet, Policy, and Test.

The question types that included several questions were then examined to determine if any significant information was being excluded by using the groupings. In all cases, there were no patterns emerging, and confidence levels within question types were very similar, indicating that using the groupings was appropriate.

DISCUSSION

A. Librarians at the QBPL are more confident answering reference questions using the Library Catalog than the Internet.

The data suggest that this hypothesis is true. Average confidence levels for questions that could be answered using the Catalog were higher than those answerable using the Internet. In comparisons by rank, the greatest difference was with Princ who demonstrate 4.3 average confidence level in answering Catalog questions while only a 3 average confidence level in answering Internet questions. GA has the smallest difference, demonstrating only a .1 point difference between Catalog and Internet questions. The other three ranks had less than 1 confidence level in difference between the two types of questions.

B. Public service librarians are more confident answering reference questions using electronic resources than non-public service librarians (control group).

The data suggest that the hypothesis is false. The Control Group demonstrated a lower confidence level in only two question types–Qgopher and Catalog. These are the two sources most commonly used by public service librarians. For most question types, the difference between Senior Librarian and the Control Group is not very significant, none being larger than 1 confidence level.

C. Branch size is a determining variable for the confidence levels of librarians in answering reference questions using electronic resources.

The data suggest that this hypothesis is false. Close examination seems to demonstrate no patterns due to the branch size of the respondents. Catalog questions demonstrated the highest confidence level for all branch sizes, with CEL showing 4.1 level and Small showing a 3.5 level. Internet questions had the next highest level of confidence, with Medium and Large having a 3.2 level while CEL and Small have a 3.3 level. Test questions were the next highest with Medium and Large showing a 3 level, and CEL and Small showing a

2.7 level. Policy questions had the lowest confidence levels, the lowest being 2 for Small and the highest being 2.9 for Medium. No real patterns could be determined from the data, and all questions showed comparative results for each branch size.

D. Position is a determining variable for the confidence levels of librarians in answering reference questions using electronic resources.

The data suggest that this hypothesis is false. Again, no patterns seemed evident from the data. Catalog questions ranged from 3.2 for J to 4.2 by ABLM/ADD. Internet questions ran from 3.1 by ABLM/ADD to 3.3 by J. Policy questions went from 3.7 by YA to 1.8 by J while Test questions ranged from a high of 3.8 by ABLM/ADD to a low of 2.9 by J.

E. Rank is a determining variable for the confidence levels of librarians in answering reference questions using electronic resources.

The data suggest that this hypothesis is false. Close examination seems to demonstrate no patterns due to the rank of the respondents. Catalog questions showed some differences from a high of 4.3 by Princ to a low of 3.4 by GA, but as in all other analysis, Catalog questions continue to have the highest confidence level. Internet questions were all about at level 3 with GA showing a high of 3.3, and both Super and Princ a low of 3 exactly. Policy questions went from level 2 for Princ to level 3 for Trainee while Test questions showed 3.4 for Trainee and 2.8 for Super.

F. Test questions will have a lower confidence levels than all other question types.

Test questions were not lower than all other question types. Both PC and Policy questions were lower than Test questions. Trainees demonstrate a lower confidence level for Internet questions than Test questions but not by much. Their average confidence level for Test questions was 3.4 while for Internet questions it was 3.1. ABLM/ADD demonstrate an extremely high confidence level for Test questions compared to all other positions, but it is only a difference of approximately 1 level.

OTHER COMMENTS FROM THE DATA

Although the data do not support all the initial hypotheses, the data provide interesting insights into the confidence levels of public service librarians when answering reference questions using electronic sources.

Control Group

First, it is interesting to note the similarities between the Control Group of non-public service librarians and public service librarians. This indicates that all librarians are expressing similar confidence levels. The distribution of questions is quite similar to those in other comparisons. Catalog questions are always highest while Policy questions remain the lowest. The initial expectation was that public service librarians would be more familiar with and confident using electronic resources as they do have the capability to use them every day at the reference desk. These results indicate that this perceived advantage does not exist. All librarians, whether public service or not, are at a similar confidence level.

Test Questions

Second, examination of confidence levels for the Test questions indicates some interesting insights. The Test questions consist of seven questions which range from difficult to impossible to complete using electronic resources. It was thought that individuals would recognize these difficult questions and rank them much lower. These Test questions would then be a measure of whether respondents answered based on actual experience or on opinion. The Test questions were ranked lower than other question types. However, Question 17 did rank fairly high. This question was to find today's temperature in Nicaragua; something that at the time of the survey was virtually impossible to locate due to the size and inaccessibility of the country itself. However, temperatures of other areas of the world were relatively easy to find. Unless one actually tried to answer the questions, it may be considered easy even by a seasoned Internet searcher.

Question 7 scored very low. This question asked about finding a person's e-mail address. This is a common discussion on the Internet, and most people familiar with the Internet would know how difficult this might be to find.

Both of the above questions were answered in a predictable fashion. Question 30, however, was not. This particular question was about locating articles about the Holocaust Myth in German. This was very difficult because, at the time, none of the search engines recognized German words. Finding articles is equally as difficult. However, this question had very high confidence levels compared to other Test Questions. It may demonstrate what respondents perceive is available using electronic resources.

Branch Size

Although no patterns were distinguishable using Branch Size as a variable, some interesting points were evident. CEL demonstrated a higher confidence level in answering Catalog questions. This is reasonable. Answers to several of the Catalog questions could be found using InfoLinQ, an OPAC, which, at the time was available only at CEL. Catalog questions are always the highest while Policy questions are always the lowest. Test questions are only slightly lower than Internet questions.

CEL respondents also demonstrated a much lower confidence level with the E-mail question. The FTP question also showed much variation with Small and CEL showing much lower confidence levels than Medium and Large. Medium also demonstrated a higher confidence level for the Policy and PC questions.

Rank

GA respondents demonstrated a low confidence level on Catalog questions compared to other ranks while Princ respondents had quite a high level. Interestingly, when it came to Internet questions, GA respondents had the highest level while Princ respondents had the lowest. Indeed, GA respondents indicated a very similar confidence level for both types of questions.

Position

The most interesting result from analysis by Position indicates that J Librarians have an extremely low confidence level on the Policy questions, one of which asked about dealing with a parent who was concerned with descriptions of oral sex on the Internet. As J Librarians are most likely to be the individuals who would have to answer such a question, it is interesting to note their low confidence level to do so.

ABLM/ADD demonstrated the highest confidence level in answering Internet questions but also the highest in answering the Test Questions. This may indicate a high level of confidence but without the experience to judge whether questions can actually be answered.

CONCLUSIONS AND QUESTIONS FOR FURTHER STUDY

All librarians demonstrate a fairly low confidence level in using the Internet in February 1996. Access to computers appears to make some difference in confidence levels as both of the groups with access to the most technology available at the time of the survey, non-public service librarians and public service librarians in the Central Library, show greater confidence.

Currently, all agencies at the Queens Borough Public Library have public and staff access to the Internet and additional databases using Netscape. It is hypothesized that there is a significant increase in the confidence levels of all librarians in using electronic reference sources due to this easier to use additional access. In March 1998, the Iteam developed a follow-up survey with a similar methodology to measure this hypothesis. This new survey takes into account changes in technology and additional databases available at QBPL. Upon conclusion, the Iteam expects to determine which resources are being used by public service librarians. The results will be compared to this survey and are expected to be available by March 1999.

Index